To everyone I have ever known;

Some more than others

Other unpublished works by this author:

Transforming Education, One Louis Vuitton Purse at a Time

Nobody Cares it's Your Birthday

Library of Congress Control Number: 201991629

What the F@&k is Wrong with Everybody Else?

What They Didn't Teach You in Business School

By David Ramsden-Wood (DRW)

Author's Note

Inspired by true events, I wrote this manuscript in 2012 as I embarked on the first part of my entrepreneurial journey. Unbelievably, that was 7 years ago. Before the LinkedIn #hottakeoftheday; before we sold one of the companies I co-founded and certainly before I had any idea how this journey would turn out.

I have long debated how to present the story now that so much time has passed. I was very introspective and grew a lot writing this book and so while I've continued to grow and there are some tweaks I would love to make; I know that would be disingenuous to the journey. And so, to preserve the authenticity of the lessons learned, I have not altered or deleted any of the content. However, to provide context to some of the key concepts, I have added some clearly identified 2019 edits where appropriate. [*This will be your cue!*]

The names and places have been changed to protect the innocent (and in some cases, not so innocent). To those who recognize themselves in some of the stories and don't like the portrayal… write your own F@&King book.

Finally, to quote my mother (without whom I wouldn't be here and from whom I developed a love of writing): "This book is about rebirth and regrowth. Your career may be a river, but life is a series of new beginnings, new chapters, new learnings and new experiences." I couldn't agree more.

Love and hugs,

DRW

Chapter 1

Losing Weight

Eat less. Exercise more.

Yes, it is that easy.

Chapter 2

Why (the F@&K) Did I Write this Book?

This book started as a title and a first chapter. It's not the best reason to start writing a book, I grant you, but it does explain a few things--namely, the title and the first chapter.

My original plan had 152 pages, 151 of which were blank. It had a red cover with white lettering, and I was going to change my name to John Collins - that way, my book would be on the shelf beside Jim Collins' *Good to Great.* It would give readers quite the alternative. No matter how badly my day had gone, the thought of my book sitting in the store right beside his always made me laugh out loud. Some days, laughter is the only link to sanity, and unfortunately, I was having *those* days a lot.

To be honest with you (which may be a bit early in our relationship), I didn't realize that my journey from where I was to where I am today would have changed me so completely – it turns out, the things they don't teach you in business school can fill a book.

But I'm getting ahead of myself. Two years ago, I had only a title, a first chapter and my mental image of my imaginary best friend John Collins. Completely by accident, I discovered that a side benefit of writing a book, or at the very least pretending to write one, was that I could credibly call myself an author (credibility is important, or so I'm told by those who are credible). As it turns out, it is far easier to talk with people at parties when you introduce yourself as an author writing a book instead of as an engineer with an MBA. Both are credible, but the latter tends to be like saying you have a contagious disease that, while aggressive and obnoxious, is manageable most of the time.

As an author, I was interesting. The things I said were made *more* interesting, and most importantly, I developed an eccentric catch phrase: "*This*…. will be a chapter in my book!" It was great at parties and I found it to be significantly less dangerous than lighting alcohol in my mouth on fire while a stranger sprinkled cinnamon over the flame, creating the illusion of a volcano. Before becoming an "author", a flamboyant party trick was standard fare - on especially difficult nights with people who didn't appreciate my "uniqueness", I would drop into the splits and perform the human worm across the room for good measure. It certainly livens up a wedding of mostly Spanish speaking guests who spent most of the night listening to speeches they didn't understand. (Jarrett, I now admit that beginning to strip was a little bit over the top- I'm sorry).

Overall, I found that the catch phrase to be far less exhausting and more universally effective at breaking tension, punctuating an event and, most importantly, not ending up in the hospital with a damaged ACL, explaining to a doctor why a grown man was doing the splits at a party.

Ah, the catch phrase. You would be surprised how nice it is to have a catch phrase.

"You're fired!"

No matter the circumstance, it fits. Ask one of your children to pass you the remote and they can't find it. "You're fired!" Works perfectly. "Let's go for a hike." "You're fired!" *[It turns out that even one as outlandish as this one can land you in the White House]*

That's why they call it a catch phrase.

"Bam!!"

Again, extremely useful. You can use it while adding some exotic spice to food. Or, less conventional but still extremely effective, you can use it while you vacuum the carpet and your spouse is watching. "Bam!!" Always good for a smile (even though it doesn't make any sense) no matter how much trouble you got into before you started vacuuming.

But let's not get carried away. Events don't always warrant a chapter, so saying it is a bit of an exaggeration.

A person performing Madame Butterfly, loudly, on a public bus while doing an interpretive dance would only get a sentence.

A person on an airplane, twelve rows back, snoring so loudly that the entire plane could hear, would warrant a paragraph. Literally, everyone on the plane would shudder in surprise every thirty seconds or so. I am not kidding you. I can't make this up. Until I heard it, it had never occurred to me that this would be possible. It sounded like a pig eating a monkey and it is a sound that will haunt me every day until the day I die.

Being an author, I turned to the person sitting beside me and said, "*This* will be a chapter in my book." Having not ever spoken to her before, she looked puzzled, reflecting on the event that led to the statement I had made.

"What's your book about?"

"What the F@&K is Wrong with Everyone Else."

"Sounds like an interesting book."

We'll see.

***

Unfortunately, as it turns out the people whom you have told that you are "an author writing a book" also think it's cool that you are writing a book and therefore introduce you to people <u>they</u> know.

"This is David, he's writing a book. He said I'm going to be a chapter!" Laughter ensues…mostly by the person making the introduction and certainly not realizing that usually, you <u>do not</u> want to be a topic in the kind of book I was writing.

Nonetheless, my pretend hobby was becoming a problem for me--especially as my social circle was beginning to shrink- I started seeing the same people over and over again. Like - at school drop off. Or work. That sort of thing. Trust me, it's really annoying.

"How's your book coming?" I always dreaded that moment.

Eyes would turn to me and all I could do was return a blank stare. Feeling the need to provide insight into the imaginary writing process, I elaborated. "Still working on the first chapter. I have to get it just right. I'm a perfectionist."

"Want me to read it?"

Um, no.

"Do you want to donate some copies to the school auction to help us raise money to make our children smarter, happier, and more productive?"

Ugh.

Apparently, in the minds of most, you have to actually publish a book to be considered an author. This was becoming an unfortunate obstacle for without a book, you are not an author but a writer, which, when it comes to parties, is more like having a terminal disease than a contagious one.

"Oh, poor David. He's a writer. That's why he acts like that. So sad. Should we buy him some food?"

No, it was not good, not good at all - it was time to turn my imaginary book into a real one. And fortunately, I finally had something to write about.

Chapter 3

What the F@&K is Wrong with Everybody Else?

I remember the first time I had to fire someone. It was my first job. Ever.

Only months before, I had been sitting in class when a job application arrived on my lap, on a clipboard no less, being passed back and forth down the rows of students. It had the title "Do you want to make $10,000?" in large print at the top of the page. Yes. As a matter of fact, I do. And so began the process where I became the manager of a university student painting business.

I had also never managed anyone before. In fact, I'd never painted before. Not even as a kid. Not even on paper. But really, how hard could it be?

Unfortunately, what I did have was a natural ability to sell. In fairness, the product I had almost sold itself. You, said homeowner, could buy yourself hours of free time and in so doing, you, great patron, would be supporting the efforts to pay for the tuition of college students- students who were working towards a valuable and productive lifetime in society. What could feel better than that? You are a philanthropist! You are an amazing person! Of COURSE, I would be happy to provide you an estimate. No, it's no trouble. I'm just honored to provide you the opportunity. Or something to that effect.

After a frantic selling season during the winter semester of my second year in University, I had $50,000 of sales. That is why I say *unfortunate* ability to sell. My recollection was that I had the highest sales in the region by a huge margin and even if it didn't, I promise you that the *sales:ability* ratio was likely wider than all the franchises put together. Unfazed and unaware, I assumed my abilities as a manager would be equally legendary. What could possibly go wrong?

I started the summer with sixteen employees. I had interviewed and hired each one myself: my hand-picked crew. I had scheduled virtually all of my preseason sales work in May, so I actually needed sixteen employees at the beginning of the summer. Before I had any experience; before I realized that perhaps I had $50,000 sales because I had dramatically underestimated the duration of time it would take to paint a house; before I realized that perhaps I wasn't that good a salesman, just a horrible estimator.

As someone who had never managed people before, I wish someone had pulled me aside and said, "You are in for a disaster." As someone who had never painted before, I wish that someone had pulled me aside and said, "You are *really* in for a disaster." When I was young, I assumed someone was going to tell me the ins and outs of the business world and look out for me; have my best interest at heart and all that. But no one did.

Out of the sixteen employees I had when the year began, I finished the season with three. Twelve quit. Painting, it turns out, is not that much fun. Sixteen minus three is…. thirteen. And then there was one.

Unfortunately, I had to fire him. For a nineteen-year-old painting franchise manager, "had to" is a strong statement. I wasn't exactly hiring for the most complicated job in the world. However, David was a special circumstance (and no, this isn't secretly a story about me, his name really was David.)

I sent him to paint. He spilled a five-gallon pail on the customer's driveway.

I sent him to sand. He broke a window.

I sent him to power wash a deck with chemicals. You know, the chemicals that strip the paint off previously painted wood so that you can repaint it? *THOSE* chemicals.

I don't know that I will ever forget that conversation.

Me: "Hey David, how are you? Did you get that deck done today?"

David: "Oh yeah; went great; the paint came right off. That stuff is crazy! I wouldn't want to spill it."

Me: "No, you wouldn't want to spill it. You ready to do it again tomorrow? I have another customer ready to go!"

Him: "Absolutely. I can't wait. I really like this job."

I will admit there was a moment of profound pride. I hung up the phone and stood there smiling. I had turned a problem employee into a success story. I had found his greatness and it was clear to me, at that moment, I could conquer the world. Sales, operations, AND management skills? In one body?! Somebody catch me because I'm going to faint!

My euphoria and excitement about my natural leadership and looming greatness lasted about thirty minutes; the planning for my bright future broken only by the sound of my phone ringing in the present.

Me: "Hello?"

Customer: "David, it's Bob. How are you?"

Me: "Great. How's the deck looking? Ready for a new coat of paint?"

Customer: "That's actually why I'm calling. I haven't seen anyone show up yet."

Me: "................."

Customer: "Hello?"

Me: "Right. Hi. No, I'm here. So, to be clear, your deck is not stripped of paint and no one has been to your house?"

Customer (out loud): "Yes. That's what I said."

Me (Out loud): "I will get right on that and send someone over right away."

Me (In my head): F@&K!!!!!!!!!!!!!!

In circumstances like this, hope is a powerful emotion. Please, don't let me have lost my house keys. I'll just check my pocket again.

Me: "Hey David, it's David. How are you doing?"

David: "Hi. Good, thanks. You?"

Me: "You know, I've been better, actually. Hey, could you tell me the address you went to this morning?"

David: "Sure can, I have it right here 4983 Forest."

Me: "Actually, I was hoping you went to 4893 Forest."

David: "Nope. Definitely 4983."

I sent him to power wash. He power washed the wrong deck.

I am not kidding. This really happened. I hung up the phone and I started to cry. The event punctuated the worst summer of my life--a summer in which I did not pass go and I did not collect $10,000. I underestimated, over employed, under delivered and made virtually no money.

I fired him. Lucky number 13.

Seriously. What the F@&K was wrong with him?

***

I remember sitting in my first meeting as a new graduate, second job, one day out of school, sitting across from a forty-year veteran of the industry--the veteran who was going to be my mentor--who also happened to be nodding off in a meeting. I say nodding off; I mean nodding. With the head bob! A head bob!! I thought I had seen the last of it in college. Apparently not.

You know the head bob, don't you? The one you saw classmates execute with precision in 8 a.m. classes?! Eyes start to droop; mouth starts to open. It's slow at first but you can see it developing; the head moves forward, imperceptibly at first and then it returns to its original position. Moments later, it moves again. Faster, and with greater depth; forward, back; forward, back, but with greater and greater depth; a crescendo. Finally, the moment has arrived! The head moves almost parallel to the floor and then "Snap!" Eyes wide open; startled; sometimes drool. Whiplash proportions. We used to play bingo in class to see who would be the first to wake himself up. It used to be funny. It used to be a drinking game for shots after class. Now, however, I was appalled.

"This is our career!" I wanted to shout. "We are here to add value every day! I am dedicated to this job making a third of the salary you are, and you are falling asleep?!" After the meeting was over, I called my boss aside.

Yes, that's right. I called my boss aside. I needed to; you see. That this engineer was to be my mentor was too much for me to take. "I cannot possibly be mentored by someone who so clearly is not committed to the company."

I strongly recommended, quite loudly and in the hall, that this individual be fired. I had seen it before. Employees who didn't fit in and didn't have the right skill set might power wash the wrong deck! And let me tell you, when that happens, you have to deal with it! It's far better to avoid the situation and fire him before it's too late—forty-one years too late!

What the F@&K was wrong with him?

He did leave the company shortly after; I never knew if he was fired.

***

I remember the first week of my MBA, where the class was discussing a case study of some veritable company through the lens of *Good to Great*, knowing full well it was the truth, the whole truth, and nothing but the truth. It's a great book, red cover and all. Companies can become great, and oh, by the way, they are built to last. But sometimes, the mighty fall.

The class discussion was lively. MBA classes are characterized by a moderator, the professor, and a group of pretty important people, the students, sharing their pretty important opinions on the subject (at least in our own minds).

When I was given the floor, after about ten students had offered gentile musings, I answered the question. Answered it. My take on *Good to Great* was pretty educated; I had read the book, not once but twice! There needed to be no more discussion. Case study solved. Final word spoken. Take a bow. Yes, I do guest lectures. Autographs? Gladly.

That was until the investment banker in the seat behind me said "You know, companies aren't built to exist throughout time. They do well until they fail and then they should be gobbled up by somebody better suited to compete in the new business climate. Everyone at the acquired company should lose their jobs and the company should die."

Utter disbelief. Did you not read the book *Built to Last*?!? I was shocked! What the F@&K was wrong with him? Investment banker. Typical.

Who admitted him into this school? We have a reputation to uphold! He dropped out of the program a few months in; apparently, he was busy on some merger he was putting together with his company.

***

I remember the first job I ever left. I had had a fantastic run at the company--almost ten years and I was fortunate enough while there to have been promoted frequently into bigger and better roles. I moved to Denver, my MBA was paid for, I learned a lot, and like to think I added a lot of value.

It was a huge independent oil and gas company--huge being the operative word. I have always believed that working at a big company is an extremely important part of anyone's career and that everyone, if you are able, should start their career with one. I believed this because I had had great advice from my father when I was about sixteen: "Until you understand why a big company has bureaucracy, you aren't ready to leave."

For someone who graduated university with the belief they could and would be running ExxonMobil within five years, this was some sort of yogic Zen statement. I didn't understand it but I felt it must hold the key to the universe, so I lived by it.

He also said: "You should never be paid as much as you're worth."

Though less yogic, it was equally profound. Early in your career, job growth far outpaces salary growth. When your salary has caught up, it means you haven't been promoted in a long time and it therefore means you are likely done with being upwardly mobile. Easy to understand and very easy to validate; if you feel you are undervalued, congratulations, you are successful.

Finally, in the *advice-that-sticks* trifecta: It's time to leave when someone taps you on the shoulder and says, "You aren't going any higher here." Now, of course it's worth acknowledging that not everyone aspires to constantly climb the corporate ladder and are perfectly happy and successful to plateau. I was not, rightly or wrongly, and so the "shoulder tap" was a pivotal learning in my life.

So, when simultaneously, I understood bureaucracy, I was dramatically underpaid, and my best friend told me I wasn't going any higher, I got a job offer and resigned to my boss. I told him I had been hired to run the operations for a different company and that I had been transitioning my role to my staff over the past two weeks but I wanted to stay for the next four weeks to ensure the transition went smoothly and the company wouldn't miss a beat.

There was no fanfare. No begging for one of their top performers to stay. I did, however get walked out the door and had a pretty flimsy exit interview with one of the junior staffers in human resources. What the F@&K was wrong with them?

From a high potential future leader to walked out the front door in the span of a day. Ridiculous.

***

I remember when I was at a football game with one of my best friends, Chad. The young man seated beside us was with two young women. I couldn't characterize the relationship, but he was certainly trying to impress one, if not both, of them. Ah, I remember those days. At least I think I remember them.

Chad likes to wear loud "Welcome to Florida" shorts. They are his own personal "F@&K You" to the world, and he got them on sale, which allows him to own a lot of pairs. As he got up to get us beers and then again when he came back, the young man seated next to us would try and impress his lady friends with some colorful comments about the shorts. I'm sure he thought he was quite hilarious.

What he did not know was that my friend grew up in Staten Island. He is the only person I know from Staten Island so he is my character reference for the place, much like the cast of the *Jersey Shore* and the *Sopranos* have given me deep insight into the culture of that particular part of the East Coast of the United States.

Near as I can tell, you don't want to mess with people from Staten Island, regardless of how they are dressed. I know not to mess with Chad. I know this because I know that Chad's brother used to collect gambling debts for some pretty shady people in Staten Island; Chad used to carry a concealed weapon for protection; Chad's brother who is significantly older and therefore bigger than Chad, broke Chad's nose three or four times in fights and once, his brother woke Chad up by hitting him with a bat across the chest. In fairness to Chad's brother, he had put a phone book on Chad's chest to prevent the bat from leaving bruises, so that was nice because bruises can be unsightly. As the saying goes, "That which doesn't kill you, makes you stronger" and Chad definitely is "stronger".

So even though Chad left Staten Island to become one of the most pleasant, successful, and smart energy executives that I know, the old adage is correct, at least when it comes to him and Staten Island: You can take the boy out of Staten Island but you cannot take Staten Island out of the boy.

Once Chad had decided that he had had enough of the young man, there was no idle threat to be made. There was only a promise and it was going to end badly. The young man was not only funny, but he was tough, and he was going to show the girls that he didn't back down from a challenge. I, myself, am a painter, not a fighter, as you can probably tell. But nonetheless, I leapt into action inserting myself between the young man and Chad. Words were exchanged. Mostly by me….offering a group hug; a bulk acquisition of colorful shorts for everyone to remember this moment by; asking the young man where I could send a wedding gift to the three of them; and quietly stating to Chad that if a punch were to be thrown that I would bravely take on the two girls.

Fortunately for me, it died down. I didn't want to have my ass kicked by a couple of girls anyway.

What the F@&K was wrong with them, anyway?

They moved seats and were never heard from again.

***

I remember having to explain to an experienced salesman that I didn't want to buy his product. Salesmen are, by nature, persistent because we customers don't always want to buy the things they have. Or in their mind, we just don't know we want to buy it *yet*. They are masters of the "up-sell", the "continual-sell" and the "add-on" sell. Witness the funeral parlor director's up-sell, as horrific and wrong as that is.

"You are going to put your mother in that? What did she ever do to you?"

"All of our premium packages come with a Bose stereo system installed in the mahogany and gold coffin."

My particular salesman was selling life insurance and there was a conflict since he also managed my money. So, while I had a modest life insurance policy through work of about $1 million dollars, it wasn't enough, apparently, in the event of my "unfortunate and untimely death" (his words). In my view, the key to life insurance is to have just enough so that your spouse--and not the salesperson--would consider your death "unfortunate and untimely." Too much insurance and you are truly worth more dead than alive and that can have negative implications. I was still worth more alive than dead and thus I slept soundly every night.

And yet, for five grueling months, my financial advisor had a fantastic life insurance plan that I couldn't live without. It was a savings plan; it was a retirement plan; it was a death plan; it was a "make you toast in the morning and rub your feet in the evening" plan. I politely listened and then said "No, thank you. I'm happy with my current plan."

A few weeks later, it was brought up again.

"Yes, I remember the life insurance. It just really doesn't fit my plans right now."

And later.

"Yes, I'm sorry about that car accident last month, people do die every day. Yes, I remember. I really don't want it."

And finally, we had the discussion for the last time.

"If I have an unfortunate and untimely death, I want to pay off the house, send my kids to college and have my wife get back on her feet. But if you think for one second that I am paying for the lifestyle of the guy that's banging my wife after I'm dead, you are f@&king crazy."

We never talked about it again. What does he think I am? An idiot? Stop selling me.

***

I remember when I was fired. What the F@&K is wrong with.... Oh.

Shit.

Chapter 4

It's Like Having Kids…

Have you ever been fired?

While the polite thing for me to say is "I hope not", that's not actually how I feel about it – I actually kind of hope you have been. Not because I'm being petty in a "misery loves company" kind of way but because it's a pretty humbling and eye-opening experience. Can you even imagine my ego before being fired?

Now, if you have been fired, I hope that it's happened only once. Personally, and I say this having put significant thought into the subject, I think one firing per lifetime is enough. Maybe even one firing per family would be acceptable; you can even include your in-laws if you'd like.

Now, it's important to acknowledge that the "HR" thing to say is here is that there is a difference between being fired, laid off, downsized and severed (or, in politically correct terms, involuntarily separated). But tomato, tomato (you have to say that one in your head for it to make any sense) - one person's firing is another person's severing. For me, firing is what happens when there exists a disagreement in direction at the senior levels of the company, and you, the junior of that team, are the one who discovers what it means to be fired.

I'm sure there are other events in life that are equally impactful, but none that influence your day-to-day life quite so drastically. After all, we spend more awake time at work than we do anywhere else in our adult lives. I realized how much time I spent at work when I came home to a family I had not spent much time with over the course of the previous few years and had to sit down and explain why starting at midnight that night, they were no longer covered by reasonable cost health care and why, in spite of years of absence, I would not be going back to work tomorrow because I no longer worked there.

"The Event", as I refer to it (even more politically correct than involuntary separation), is a massive shock to your soul. Nothing says failure quite like the termination of income when you have a mortgage, a wife who gave up her career to raise kids so that you could have one, and a four and a six year old who know you live with them, but aren't totally sure what your role is. It lends perspective to where you are in life, how you define yourself, and gives you the opportunity (which when written in mandarin is the same character as crisis) to reset and chart a new course. I did not have this perspective in the days and weeks that followed but the sun did rise, life did go on, and for the first time in a very long time, I was forced to look at my life and evaluate it for what it was, not what I had planned on it being a few short weeks prior. I believe that few other things in life allow you to do that.

If you haven't been fired, I don't think that you totally understand what I'm saying. People learn best by doing, or in this case, by being done. In my big company days, I had fired more than my fair share of people in the time leading up to it, but

I didn't understand it until I experienced it myself. I liked to think I did it better, but fired is fired, like dead is dead.

So, I imagine if you have never been fired, you are going to smile, but maybe not entirely absorb what I'm saying. Regardless, I will still share my learnings with you because being fired was a huge turning point for me, and, well, I like you. I really like you. You bought my book and you are now thirty or so pages into it. Accordingly, if I can help you so I can be the in-law you take credit for and you don't have to be fired to find happiness in your new course, then it was worth it. Both the $199 dollars for the book and the couple of hours you spent reading it.

WHAT?!? I can't sell this for $199? What if it comes with an iPhone?

Oh. OK. No iPhone? $75 it is.

***

The best analogy I can think to use is that it's like when your friends start having kids after you have your own little prodigies. You tell your friends to enjoy each other before "The Big Day", to go out for dinner often, to have friends over, to travel, to enjoy their sleep, because things are going to change dramatically when baby makes three.

They smile and listen politely, but they don't believe you because, for them, parenthood will be different. They will experience childhood in a totally different way than anyone else. They will go for dinner, travel, not talk constantly about their child's bowel movements, and under no circumstances will they become "those parents."

Yeah, okay. Let me know how that goes for you.

After two years, you see them again, for probably the second time. Of course, you saw them five days after the baby was born and you brought them a baby gift: a toy that sings annoying songs and can't be turned off without taking the battery out which is hard to do because the batteries are hidden inside the toy and you need a Philips screwdriver to get to them. They did, after all, get you a similar toy.

For years, you have invited them to your parties, out to dinner, to movies, and once you even had a trip planned to the mountains. Unfortunately, they couldn't make it. It was almost inexplicable, and certainly surprising. They were, after all, going to experience childhood in an entirely different way than everybody else.

And then, after two years, they invite you to dinner. Amazing! You hug, they serve you wine, but you notice the matriarch isn't drinking. You have small talk. You have dinner. You know where this is going.

"Great news, we are so excited, we are having baby number two."

You smile. Having two kids of your own, you strongly consider not saying anything. It didn't work last time, but you are friends, and they have now learned through experience that you are wise and learned. You say, "Double the kids are four times the work, give or take."

Of course, they smile, but they don't believe you. Because it will be DIFFERENT for them for baby number two.

Yeah, okay. Let me know how that goes for you.

Chapter 5

Ouch.

The days that followed "The Event" were the hardest few days of my life. That I remember particularly clearly.

I had been stressed out, miserable, and working sixteen-hour days, seven days a week--by choice of course--in the months and maybe years leading up to it, but nothing could compare to how I felt in the days that followed.

In my mind, January 31st (the day before I got fired), I had purpose; I knew what 6:15 a.m. meant. I knew what I was going to do every day, with every crisis. I was important. I was creating millions of dollars of value every single day for the organization in an asset I had built from scratch. I was the captain, with two or three trusted lieutenants, and we had answers to everything. And then, it was gone.

Healthcare taken away at midnight; no place to go during the day; absolutely no idea what I was going to do. I went from a job that pulled me in twenty different directions all simultaneously that I had willingly sacrificed my personal life for to absolutely nothing.

As I write this today, I am appalled to know that is how I felt, but I know it to be true.

There were two little boys who hadn't seen their father in years and wasn't particularly present when they did see me because I had worked myself literally to death. And now I didn't even have a job to show for it. Don't worry boys, University is overrated anyway.

I had a wife at home who had given up her job, moved countries, and endured some pretty tough times with the husband she had--a husband who was significantly different than the one she had chosen to marry--watching the two little boys. "'Til death do us part," they say. And she was strongly contemplating the "death" part for me.

A few weeks prior to "The Event", I had told my wife that I wouldn't be joining our family on a ten-day trip to Hawaii, a trip that had been booked for over a year beforehand. My reason: I couldn't be away from work for that long.

Her entire family was going. I wasn't. Divorce was imminent and I didn't care. I surmised with 100% confidence that she was planning on packing the kids up and moving back to Canada upon her return from Hawaii. I also knew that I was staying in Denver to continue my career. Some might say I'm exaggerating the divorce part since I have been known to embellish on occasion. So it is important to know that I have subsequently confirmed that this was, in fact, the case. My wife and kids would have passed go (in this case Denver) and collected a few hundred (thousand) dollars on their way back to Canada, for good.

And then, "The Event" happened.

For me, my first thought was not of my life, my family, or the free time I was about to have. It was not about the relief that I should feel now that I would no longer have to fight every day at the office with people who took for granted what I did for the company. It was not even about the inequity that I was the one who had been fired despite the fact that only myself, and my right hand person, Elisa (and a very few other extremely capable and talented people on my team) had executed a $500 million dollar transaction that was the company's biggest asset and was investing into it another $300 million a year.

No. It was that I wouldn't be going to work on February 2nd. No emails. No phone calls. No meetings. No decisions. No lunches with salesmen. No dinners with vendors. It would be just my family--the four of us--in a house we could no longer afford, looking at each other with the three of them wondering, "Who is this guy sitting across from us on the couch and why does he look so blue?" Get it… *Avatar*? Never mind.

There is no dispute that I had gotten myself into the mess that I eventually got fired out of. I had chosen to take a stand against those that "didn't care" about the company or the capital that we invested. The pinnacle event didn't come in the days that led up to the event; it actually transpired a full six months beforehand. We had invested $500 million in an acquisition and my peer and *her team* didn't manage the back-office details and didn't realize that 20% of the asset was, in short order, to be written down to zero. An entirely preventable occurrence; an occurrence that could have been avoided with even the slightest bit of interest in doing their job; but the interest waned, and the occurrence was imminent.

When I discovered their mistake on a Friday, I called for an all hands-on deck, all weekend effort to come up with solutions by Monday. Elisa, of course, worked all weekend to come up with a solution- a solution that did actually preserve $100 million of value when we implemented it.

My *peer's team* didn't spend a minute on it and showed up Monday as though nothing was wrong. That was the final straw for me. Had *they* dropped everything and gone in and made last ditch efforts over the weekend on how this could be salvaged, I could have dealt with that. But they didn't and I lost it. It's one of the few times in my career when I have ever been "angry." I fired one and two resigned, but not immediately and not nearly soon enough. The infighting began shortly thereafter; I was imputed as the reason for my peer's resignation and the deck was set. All firings are the result of a string of events, but it only takes one to really put it into motion. In my case, this was the beginning and it was to be 5 months before the end.

The fact that my replacement and my former boss left the company within 6 weeks of my departure should have been solace, but it didn't get me my job back. It didn't get my bonus back. It didn't take away the asset I built into two billion dollars from the same company that fired me. No. On February 2nd, life went on as it had February 1st for everyone else, just not me. It's a tangled web we weave, and most of the time you can only see the path in hindsight (or worse, you see it soon, but not soon enough and there isn't anything you can do to change course).

I am quite confident there were a number of people on both sides of the aisle that cheered that day. Those that I pushed at work--the "B-" and "C" players that I, quite frankly, could have been more patient with--cheered because I was gone, and their daily lives got easier. Karma, payback and the hubris police had simultaneously caught me and in the world, there was "justice." "Work isn't everything, calm the F@&K down." "I just want to do my job and go home." "Leave me alone. And stop emailing me at 8:30 at night, it's stressing me out."

Those that were closest to me cheered too, much more quietly of course, but hopeful that the David that I used to be would return and the person that I had become would be rocketed back to outer space. Remember that guy that power washed the deck? That was funny. Tell that story again, it always makes me laugh when you tell it. Why don't you tell it that way anymore? Please come back.

The job, my career, and the choices I had made had morphed who I was. In the opening chapters, I characterized it as unhappy. We didn't know each other that well back then. I feel now like our relationship has really grown, so I can say it: I was an asshole. Not a mean asshole. Just a one-dimensional, self-important, confused asshole. And I'm pretty sure I wasn't going to change. So, it is ironic, of course, that being fired saved what little of my personal life I had left. It is also the reason for which I now drop my kids off at school every day, coach them in hockey, head the fundraising efforts for their school and am on the PTA. But more on that later.

The next day, I got up just like I did every other workday with a few small differences: My eyes were red. I was hollowed out from the inside. I hurt and I had absolutely no place to go.

So, I put on my suit, went downtown and had coffee with, I don't know, fifteen or twenty people? All of whom were former colleagues.

From some, I was looking for validation; from some I was hoping for a job offer. But more than anything, I needed to get back in control of my life and this seemed like a pretty good place to start. I ended up extremely over-caffeinated. I ended the worst day of my life, went home and started really writing.

I now know that being fired was the best thing that ever happened to me. At the time, I didn't have that perspective. I did, however, have anger. I needed validation of myself and a structure for anger. I needed an outlet. And fortunately, I had a killer title and first chapter. I'm thankful I did.

I wrote the next two chapters in the days that followed. I didn't have anything else going on.

Chapter 6

Leaving (or Being Left by) a Job

There are fifty ways to leave your lover but only three ways to leave a job: Gloating about the new job, fuming about the company you are leaving, or with your head held high. I believe that while the circumstances may differ, these are the only three ways. I have only left three companies in my career and I have now departed in all three ways. Only one of these is acceptable.

The first time was five years into my career, an intercompany transfer from Anadarko's Canadian office to their U.S. office in Denver after the Canadian Division was sold. Let's call it, Anadarko Part I.

Four hundred and fifty people, all of whom knew their life was going to change the moment the deal was closed. All of whom knew that their projects, their relationships, their champions, their routines, and the source of their paycheck would change the moment the deal closed. Since we humans trade on knowledge, the announcement that they were selling Canada was as good as the announcement that we were sold. And here I was--one of four people--including the Canadian President, Mike, himself a transplant from the Houston office to Calgary, who was offered a transfer to the U.S. office. Four. Out of four hundred and fifty people. I must really be great.

For the next forty-five days, I was talking to my new bosses who knew all my old bosses, knew all of my projects, and knew all of my champions and accomplishments. I was looking for houses, figuring out my ninety-day plan in the new job, and I was pumped. Twenty-eight years old and promoted to the management team in Denver after a $24 billion cash acquisition of two firms in one day! I worked for the best company ever!

Yet everywhere around me were the people I had worked with for five years. Their projects came to a complete halt. People were going through the motions; applying for other jobs; scared for their current job; and they were mad at me. What the F@&K was wrong with these people? Didn't they realize I was getting a transfer to a great opportunity with this amazing company that just…

Oh. Check. Don't gloat.

At the same time I noticed three managers, whose strengths I didn't appreciate at the time (they weren't being transferred, after all, how good could they be?), were going door-to-door telling people to use their offices as their resume. "Turn all your projects into presentations!" they said. Deadlines; signing authorities; pressure to deliver. All had vanished instantaneously and all that was left was time. You can't hope that things will be okay. Hope is not a plan.

But, having time meant being able to be out ahead of "the important", not just reacting to "the urgent" and "on fire." Having time meant preparing to interview with the new company when they would be under pressure to reduce staff, cut costs, and make decisions in the brave new world. These managers made it a point to make sure everyone who worked there was prepared for the eventuality of the question: "So what do you do?" and the employees could tell them in the best way possible. If they don't think they need your position, it wasn't you. If they need your position, it will be you.

That was a pretty good experience. The managers who were seen to be true leaders are still deeply respected by everyone who worked there, even though only ten or so remained a year after of the transaction. I think they were fantastic, and the company lost some excellent people when they didn't offer them a transfer.

In the second act, Anadarko Part II, it turns out that the merger was my brave new world. The merger was more like a reverse takeover. Those who championed me and ultimately transferred me down to the U.S. were reorganized out within six months. Virtually all the senior management roles were filled with people from the "acquired" company. You have got to be kidding me. What the F@&K.....

The interesting thing about career trajectory (or at least the interesting thing to me) is a large part of it comes down to who your champions are and what career trajectory they are on. Some people call this "hitching your wagon to someone above you." As they get promoted, you get promoted and you can move up fairly high and fast. When the wagon in front of you is run off a cliff, you had better unlink quickly or you are likely to land on top of them, smashed to smithereens.

I did not know this at the time, and I left my wagon firmly affixed to the past and after three years, I had had enough.

Enough of not fitting the new culture; enough of hearing about my champions being trashed for what they had done; enough of being micromanaged through process implementation and meeting after meeting to discuss the summary of the meeting we had just had and which was preceded by a pre-meeting to make sure that everyone knew what would be said. At least that was my perspective at the time.

It was bullshit and I was going to let them have it. "Have it" in the work world means quit. I spend six weeks training my team to do my job; I transitioned all my duties to my direct reports; and when I resigned, I gave three weeks' notice to ensure things went smoothly. Take that, Anadarko.

As things go, companies can react to resignations in different ways. My offer to stay for three weeks was gratefully accepted and I met with my team and the extended team to tell them that I was moving companies but that it had been one of the best experiences of my life etc., etc., etc.

The next morning, senior management had decided I wasn't going to stick around for three weeks and ended my employment that afternoon. Are you kidding me?!?

I was pissed off. After all that I had endured for three years with no champions and planning to leave with a dignified exit, "they" defiled it. It hurt that after almost 10 years with the same company and having moved to an entirely different country, I wasn't trusted enough to stay the duration of my notice period. I became angry and spiteful. I wrote a letter. A six-page open letter which I read during my exit interview and left a copy for them to refer to. Take that!

Then, after being in place at my new job for only a month later, I hired someone who had worked for me at Anadarko that was a real up and coming young rock star. Let's call her Cinderella. It was a coup for me to steal her and it really pissed Anadarko and some former colleagues of mine off. But for me, it felt good. How could it not? I was so valuable to them and they didn't even know it! I was irreplaceable. The job that I did for them would have to have five people to do what I did. They were screwed! How could they be so stupid as to let me go and even walk me out the door?

Well. Things did go on.

I was replaced.

The asset was successful.

I burned a bridge with a lot of people that I really respected and worst of all, I looked petty and small. Cinderella turned into her angry stepsisters and became a frustrated, disengage employee who ditched hours and whose performance plummeted before going back to the company six months later, welcomed with open arms. Cinderella's performance went back to the way it was, and she has been extremely successful since. I put Cinderella in a company I didn't understand, with a culture that would turn out to bite the hand that fed it, and I lost a friend because I was too immature to know better.

Oh. Check. Don't be petty.

So. I got fired two days ago. That was fun. Um…. Not.

I had fired ten people in the three years leading up to this moment, so I was intimately familiar with the signs that it was coming. Infighting, resignations and scapegoating led to avoidance. For weeks leading up to "the event" my boss would schedule meetings that in the years prior had just been drop-ins.

Other people in other groups were being asked for data or answers to questions that I was responsible for. I was trying to hire four people and promote one and HR "couldn't find the time" to do the simplest of tasks. Mental note (not that one is required): These are the signs that you should be working with headhunters at a rapid pace.

And then "it" appeared. "It" was a 4:30 meeting request on a Wednesday--the day before results were to be issued to the market--a random 'Org Design' meeting invitation with Fred, my boss and Phillis, our HR person. I was at lunch and the meeting was to occur in 4 hours. Organizational design?! I declined the request. That was fun. I laugh out loud to think about that part actually.

About 15 minutes later, I got a response. "Is there a better time today we can meet?"

"Phillis. I'm not dumb."

And so, after thirty more minutes of actual calm, I walked into Phillis's office and said, "Well, let's get this over with, am I being treated fairly or am I being f@&ked?" Her face told me everything I needed to know. It turns out it was *almost* fair with a huge twist of pettiness.

Fred, my boss, whom I had deeply respected up until about five months ago when the trouble started, came in and before he could open his mouth, I said "I know why you are here, and I'm sad but I'm good with it so don't stress about the speech."

He cocked his head in that sort of surprised, sort of pleased look and said, "Well, the results aren't what they needed to be, so we need to make a change. You are a talented guy--let's take some learnings out of this. The package is X which Phillis will talk to you about. Best of luck." I had delivered that speech almost word for word ten times. Turns out, I didn't like being on the receiving end. Payback's a bitch.

In that moment, I had what many refer to as "a moment of choice." Perhaps if I hadn't known it was coming, I wouldn't have been as aware of my moment. Perhaps I would have panicked; gotten angry; yelled; been destructive; done all the things that come to mind when you are put before the metaphorical firing squad. And so, I said "I have very much appreciated the opportunity, you have a great team, I take accountability for the results and I understand the decision. I wish everyone here the best of success." I reached out, shook his hand and sat quietly waiting to understand the package.

News Flash!!!!! The package matters. A lot.

In the moments after being fired, shortly after you go into shock, the very first moment of the rest of your life is when you are told about "the package." It is all that is left of your former self; the last acknowledgement of your contribution. When someone feels treated fairly, they can feel "happy." Not "happy I just met the love of my life" or "happy I got to fly in first class" but "happy I have some security as I take the next steps in my career." With that emotion, your time with the company feels valued, important and it brings a measure of closure. Or, at least I imagine it would.

On the other hand, the emotion I got to discover was quite the opposite of "happy." I was within forty days of a fairly significant cash bonus that had been granted when I joined the company three years before, in part to entice me to leave the job I had been at previously. During my three years, I had led the team that had identified and negotiated the transactions to acquire two companies for close to six hundred million dollars. I was responsible for the integration and execution of those acquisitions and at that time of my firing, it was worth close to two billion dollars. So, what was fairly significant to me--a couple hundred thousand dollars--became the focal point of my perception of fairness. I know with a great degree of familiarity that when an employee feels the company is being petty, they don't feel valued; they don't feel important and they feel very, very mad. The package matters.

There is an awkward moment after you've been fired and after you know the package and you stand up to leave the office in which your foreseeable future has been dramatically altered: The business of leaving. Shock brings focus and focus brings awareness: How do I transfer all your contacts off my phone? How do I get a new phone? How do I access my personal files as I assume my login has been locked? Who is going to pack my office? And why is the HR person following me around everywhere I go?

I went back to my office to pack, my HR shadow in tow. I picked up the phone to call Elisa. As usual, she was in my office in fifteen seconds, as the best right-hand people usually are.

When she saw my face, she knew right away. When she saw Phillis, she was pissed. I said, "I have to pack my office, I've been fired, effective immediately." I picked up the phone again to call the rest of my team to tell them the news. For some reason it's important to be the one who tells people directly.

Phillis tried to stop me. I looked at her and said "You have to be F@&king kidding me. I'm calling my team so you can calm the F@&K down." It was the first time in a long time I was allowed to be me, call a spade a spade and ignore "the way we should act."

I called all the key people on my team; "Guys, this is going to come as a shock to you, but I have been fired effectively immediately. I don't want you guys to be mad. Or upset. Or defend me. I want you to hold your head high and do your jobs."

I started to pack my office and Elisa wouldn't let me. She and our other core team partner, Doug, packed my office. There we were, the two people that had trusted me the most; believed in me the most; and I had let down the most were going to be there for me even as I wasn't going to be there for them. It was probably the first time they had seen someone close to them fired. I suppose it's a bit like a funeral. Packing boxes with memories of the things that won't be again. I remember later when Doug told me about finding my performance review in my drawer from the year before. I had received special commendation that had ranked me as one the top employees in the company. From first to worst in 11 months. That's how fast life can change.

As they packed, I called all the assets' key people--the people without whom things would fall apart--and said "I wanted to let you know that I am leaving. The results weren't where they needed to be, and so I support the decision. The change is going to be good. I am so proud of what we have done together, and this was a reflection on my leadership, not your results, and I thank you for everything you've done, and I know you will keep doing it."

I sent a note to my staff.

All

I wish that this email was arriving under different circumstances, and, moreover, I wish I was able to get around to each of you individually and thank you personally.

Effective immediately, I will be leaving the company. 2011 was filled with a lot of wonderful accomplishments and unfortunately some noise that distracted the company from what we needed to accomplish. I wish everyone continued success in what we were doing, and I know the new direction will be positive.

My best

***

When it came time to leave, Elisa and Doug wouldn't let me leave carrying my own boxes. They walked out the front door with me shoulder to shoulder. We went to my car, put them in the trunk. Hugged. And I drove out of the parking garage for the last time.

I don't know what the F@&K is wrong with everybody else, but at that moment, it was not going to be me.

Chapter 7

When You Leave Your Job

One of the proudest moments of my adult life (that is, being mature when my career was ripped from my hands) lasted about thirty-six hours, which, I think, is the organizational incubation period for timetomoveonitis.

Timetomoveonitis is characterized by the momentum shift from the shock of the departure where supporters are saddened and quietly going back to doing their jobs and the time that the new regime steps in to fill the void. It's often difficult to pin-point the end of the gestation period, but it is usually started by someone at the company uttering the phrase "It's probably for the best." And then timetomoveonitis is unleashed--all the wrongs you have ever done, the omissions, the mistakes, the slightings, the imperfections that everybody else sees in you every day are surfaced. And then the uproar begins. It is easy to add to the noise to advance the new regimes' agenda and tada! – your legend is killed. The warm reflections are gone. History is written by the victor. Tough shit.

How can this be? Think of the American president. At any given time, the most powerful person in the world has a 50% approval rating. Forty percent of the population will hate them, no matter what they do. Forty percent will love them, no matter what they do. And the other 20% swing with the tide. Good events love him (or eventually her.) Bad events hate him. It's just the way it is.

History tends to repeat itself. Flash back five years before when all my champions were reorganized out of the company in what HR professionals like to call an "involuntary separation." All my champions were revered and then, in an instant, timetomoveonitis hit. I saw it firsthand, and yet still, I didn't expect it when it happened to me.

When I was fired, I spent twelve hours in the dumps. Lost. Rejected. Worthless. Like I let all my people down. True to form, as a fixer, I rebounded quickly. The problem was: no job. So I needed a job. Get a job. Lose the sadness. Regain the mojo. Life is good again.

Twenty-four hours in, I had a job offer that would put me back to work in a pretty exciting role two days later. (Now, let's be clear, being self-aware, some groundwork had been laid in the months before. And timing, as they say, is everything. They needed "a someone." I was that "someone." Tada! Employed!) Coupled with leaving proudly and the injustice being voiced, I was vindicated. I WAS worthwhile. I WAS found. Confirmation again that everyone else was the problem.

Leaving an organization, whether by choice or by someone else's choice, is like having a part of your soul ripped out. We spend more hours at work than we do with our family, friends, kids and most likely in the busy times, 50% more than we spend sleeping--

our second most time-consuming relationship--where you get to spend more time with lil' ol' you and your thoughts. Research says one of the keys to retention is to have a best friend at work. Departing a job leaves behind someone very close, probably two or three other "pretty closes", and a handful of other "Hey! How's your mother doing after her surgery last week?" Chances are, except for one or two, you will never work with them again. Many you may see no more than once or twice a year at industry functions, and some you will forget the name of in a few months. From every single day, fighting-the-good-fight to absolutely nothing.

This is not only work. This is school. This is church. This is life. We move on. So, while you are working through your separation issues, so too are your peers and they have to come to grips with it. And usually coming to grips with something painful, like when part of the soul is ripped out of an organization (for after all, we ALL contribute to culture), we push it away, we reject it, and we move on.

So, while some people stay icons (Steve Jobs, Bill Gates…. and not always beloved), organizations need to move on and so, part of leaving your job is accepting the chirping, the noise, and letting it pass.

Everyone, no matter what role they play, is replaceable and everyone, no matter who they are, has weaknesses. People need to rationalize behavior, no matter how bizarre. Everyone needs to make sense of things. Leaving a job must be, at its heart, about you. And therefore, it becomes about you. Soon, the noise dies down and everything is right with the world. Once the racket ceases, there will be those best friends and close friends who stay loyal and cannot accept the new regime, and they, too, will exit and the culture will pile on and say "sympathizer" and fill the void in the previous story with an even quicker dismissal.

In his book *Straight from the Gut,* Jack Welch talks about succession planning. While some of the GE management philosophies may be out of favor today, I still think he has an accurate perspective for senior leadership positions. When he was at GE and about to move on, of the fifty or so qualified candidates to take his job, he culled it down to three. To all three he said "One of you will be me. The other two are leaving the organization with a great reference. The reason? The bitterness felt by the other two and their sympathizers will undermine the ability of the new person to take the helm of the new regime. Not everyone will like the choice, and some will vehemently oppose it, but eliminating champions and their supporters moves the organization forward."

Break-ups are never fun, but former lovers and friends quickly become .... Well, nothing. Your former friends' friends are impacted, and their friends believe the story they are told because that is their job. In time, when the pain is gone, a more balanced (but not *that* balanced) memory is restored, but it takes many years to pass. And so it is in leaving a job.

What the F@&K is wrong with everyone else?

You.

Also By David Ramsden-Wood

Book Two, Chapter One

Reflection

A bit of marketing advice - people like to get more than they paid for. And in this case, you get two books for the price of one. How good is that?! You don't even need to wait the customary two years; you just keep reading. Although I grant you, $75 is pretty expensive--even for a book of this quality--so such extras should be expected.

It's also pretty fortunate because I think the answer to my question is probably a little anti-climactic. Not "Who is John Galt?" anti-climactic, but close. After two years, this book would sell even more poorly than the first one. What do you mean, "You?" What the F@&K? I am not the problem, it's everybody else. Remember the painting guy? I mean, come on!

Can you imagine coming home from work to sit on your porch, have a glass of wine and find that by some freak occurrence that **ALL** the paint on your beautiful, giant deck was just missing? Gone. There this morning, gone this evening.

You would call your neighbors and they would explain that some nice young boy pulled up in a truck, attached your hose to his power washer, and then proceeded to strip the paint off your deck, smiling and waving at the neighbors while he did it. That is some crazy vandal! What is the world coming to?!

After I fired David, I felt badly. Not too badly, of course. I have told that story for fifteen years and I still get tears streaming down my face when I do it right. There were a few years in the middle there that I didn't do it right. Long before I had the title, I knew that it would be a chapter in my book.

That he was in the wrong role, there can be no doubt. I'm sure my firing him was partly a relief. But when you are a student and you are working your way through college and money is scarce, getting fired is a significant hindrance. I'm not sure he tells the story as I do which is a good reminder that there are two sides to every story, even the funny ones.

You might be asking, as I did many, many times that summer, "How did I end up as a manager of a painting business?" Remember the clipboard? I signed myself up for this job. $10,000! Sounds great, doesn't it? What could possibly go wrong? In fact, I was walking down the street the other day and someone said "Hey, do you want to make $10,000? Really easy money." Lesson learned, I declined.

Getting "the job" was almost as clever as the recruiting method. It was exactly the same way people get you to go to the timeshare presentations. "Free Camera, all we need is thirty minutes of your time." Etiquette dictates that when someone gives us something, you give them something back, even when the values are not even close. Its why dealerships give out free coffee in hopes that you will buy their cars. It also turns out that when something is extremely hard to get, you want it more, even when having it is a huge pain in the ass. Somebody please tell Cindy Crawford I'm still not interested.

I had two interviews to get my $10,000 job. I can truthfully say that of all the interviews I've had in my life, these two were the most intense. Every question was behavioral, and the interviewers hung on every word you said while taking copious notes. The questions were all very grown-up questions--especially to someone who had never worked before.

"How would you manage a difficult employee?"

"What is your philosophy when it comes to the customer?"

"What is your leadership dogma?"

Dogma? I don't even know what that is.

After each answer I gave, they wrote. They looked at each other, sometimes with a smile, but mostly with a shake of the head. "Poor kid," they seemed to imply, "I just don't think he's good enough."

They saved the best question for last.

"How would you feel if we gave you the opportunity to work for us this summer? Tell us why you are the best candidate."

I went into full sales mode with them: "This is an amazing opportunity for me. I will be the best employee you ever have, doing all that needs to be done, better than anyone has ever done it. I will give you my heart and soul and the company will want to name an employee award after me and give scholarships to underprivileged children in my name. Heck, I might even work there after I graduate."

I still had absolutely no idea what the job was. After all this time, they had never mentioned it and I was too afraid to ask, lest I ruin my chances of employment.

After a week of waiting on pins and needles, the call came.

"Congratulations! You are one of the few successful applicants." I was ecstatic! I had wanted it so badly. They gave me their approval, and I owed them my allegiance. My future, my hopes and my dreams –everything came down to this moment.

"You will be running a painting franchise this summer."

A what? Oh, you sneaky guys, you! I'll take it! They like me!! They really like me!

In four months, I did not make the promised $10,000. The company for whom I worked, however, made $15,000. I, on the other hand, made $2,000. On $50,000 in revenue--one of the highest sales numbers in Western Canada. Forty hours per week for sixteen weeks. $2,000. $3.12 per hour, not including all the time I spent from January to April giving estimates to people, and eventually closing $50,000 worth of painting services while I was going to school. On top of that, I had to buy my own truck, ladders, and supplies, race around from job site to job site, and pay for my own gas. If I misquoted a price, which with no painting experience was apt to happen, the company still took the 30% of the revenue and I ate the difference. A good thing to remember, whether you are starting a business or investing in the stock market is that *Revenue* is not the same as *Profit.* I remember negotiating this point before I started (the only point I negotiated…or tried to negotiate): "Why was the commission not a net profit interest?" "That's just the way it is." I have hated that answer ever since.

The entire process led me to develop a deep philosophy of having transparency and directness with people who are not selling me stuff, an important clarification after that last story. I have always been very open with everyone about my intentions and my views of their career, their performance, and my expectations. Many times, I was too open and it came back to bite me more times than not. Nonetheless, I still believe in being open, direct, and upfront and I don't think that will ever change.

On the positive side, I did learn my lesson and have successfully managed to avoid purchasing anything at time share presentations. Granted, my exit strategies are not always graceful--I once feigned a mental breakdown by shouting and cursing at the sky "Stop telling me to do things! Stop it, he's a nice man. I won't!" I stood up and lumbered out, continuing to converse with the voices in my head as I went.

So that's the background about how I became a painting franchise manager. Context matters, it always does. So do intentions, good or otherwise. I was trying to make money, too. It's why they call it a summer job instead of a summer hobby.

But I digress; back to the other David. I knew, even then, that the right way to manage was to have him try every role possible and have lots of performance conversations with him along the way. It was something I did throughout my entire career, no matter how difficult the conversations were. You should always know where you stand with your supervisor and you should never be surprised with a performance rating, a promotion, or anything in between.

So, while he wasn't surprised at being fired, I never considered the possibility that perhaps I had sent him to the wrong house. Sure, there had been other mishaps, but it was possible. What was my culpability in his performance? Maybe the fact that I had sixteen employees and was running a business that I knew nothing about was a contributing circumstance.

Perhaps since I was frustrated with him, it led me to avoid him and therefore I wasn't being a good manager and having performance conversations with him. I didn't ask about his day, his family, or even where he lived. I knew nothing about him. I fired David with no malice. It's nothing personal, it's just business, right? It happens.

Flash forward fifteen years. Less funny story, at least to me. A management restructuring. Same result, different David. I started writing—and I mean *really* writing--the day I was fired. It really is a chapter in my book; quite a few chapters, actually.

Chapter Two

Who You Are and the Decisions You Make

I am not a philosopher--except when I'm drunk—and then I'm quite confident my IQ raises 20 points. *[I didn't realize I had written this at the time but is clearly the source of my #hottakeoftheday motto: Write drunk, edit sober]*

Right now, I am sober, so I refer to the declaration about not being a philosopher. However, I do think that life is about decisions. The day-to-day is great and every day is an adventure, but real life is about the choice you make to do "Option A" or "Option B". I think you can reflect on your life and see the six or eight key decisions that you made which set the stage for everything that was to follow. Where to go to school, what courses to take, where to live after you finish with school, and whether you want to focus on your career or focus on your life. Your career, in large part, stems from the decisions you make somewhat early in life--at least relative to where you are when you begin to have some notion of what it's like to be a grown-up. The rest is just luck and hard work or some arguable combination of the two.

I was very fortunate that for most of my life, and arguably my entire life until the moment I was fired, things had gone pretty well. I grew up in an upper middle-class family; I was provided with the opportunity to go to the best (public) schools; to college; to compete internationally in a sport of my choosing. And yet, when I was fired, the confidence I had; the "power" I thought I had was taken away for a long time.

Perhaps you have always defined yourself by what you are, and you don't let anything impact you in that way. I believed that I was a confident, capable, don't-care-what-anyone-else-thinks kind of a guy. But, as it turned out, I wasn't because I did, in fact, care. And because I cared, I ended up where I was, and, ultimately was fired and totally gutted. My power was with what people gave me and how people identified with me. I think quite possibly that it is that way for a lot of people. You may say that you don't care what people think of you, but you make compromises to what you believe in the name of being a good friend, a good partner, or a good employee. That, to me, is the essence of the issue. What do "you" get from being good and is it being reciprocated?

As a kid, I was brought up in an extremely high-achieving family and I idolized my dad. He was the best man in my wedding, and he is, to this day, my hero. He's also still alive and at some point, will be among the first to read this, because that's just the way we are, so I should say it: I love you, Dad.

When I found out that my father--perhaps the smartest person I know--didn't go to many fourth-year engineering classes while he was getting his degree and that my mother, in her first year of education, went to his classes to take notes…Well, this was a call to arms!

I, David, could one up that. I decided that I wouldn't do the assignments! Even during my first year, I decided that I wouldn't go to many classes, I would learn all the course material the week of the exam, show up and take the exam, and pass. At my University, as a reward for dedication and improvement during the year, if you did better on your final than on the rest of your course material, then that would be the grade you received for the class. I did not respond in the intended way to that compensatory system.

I am convinced that I am the first person to almost fail out not for partying too hard, but for trying to prove that I was the smartest guy in the room. I'm not. This story serves as exhibits A – Z of that. I am pretty smart--not in all things--but at math, numbers, science, and things of that realm. I have a recollection of numbers (i.e. phone numbers of lots of kids I knew when I was five); I can go through financial statements and recite the major numbers from memory, that kind of thing. It's a blessing. And I totally threw it away.

With more perspective, I'm going to chalk it up to learning style. Everyone has a learning style; a favorite work method; a preferred work environment. You need to know what your learning style is and equally important, be aware of the learning styles of others. When you see someone acting out, I suggest that it is a way of exhibiting rejection to a teaching style and I think it can be avoided with good observation and mentoring.

If you can believe it, during my first year of college classes, I dropped out of a chemistry course after the initial lecture because I read the syllabus and discovered that I had taken it already while in the International Baccalaureate program in high school. Instead of thinking "Wow, that's great! I get a course that will be easy, and I will get great marks!", I instead said, "This is an insult to my intelligence!", went to the registrar, and dropped the course. It wasn't until weeks later that I discovered that I couldn't challenge the exam and get credit. They wouldn't let me re-register and that chemistry class conflicted with a core course every year from that point forward. It was the single factor that led me to having to get my degree over six years, not four.

This unfortunately did not lead to increased conformity. Instead, it led to even more rebellion against the system that was University. Seriously, what the F@&K was wrong with me? Oh, hold on, I mean everybody else?

I got an F in an electrical engineering course because I didn't like it, so I never went to class and, quite frankly, didn't understand it. Those electrical engineers are smart! Fortunately, or so I thought, my girlfriend in college was an electrical engineer a year ahead of me so I presumed that she could tutor me before the exam, and I would do fine. Incorrect. It was an open book exam. As it turns out, if you must open your book during a 3-hour exam, you are in trouble. I was in trouble.

Miraculously, but with a poor GPA, I made it to third year. I decided I didn't want to be a painting franchise manager so I had absorbed a little bit in those first two years, but not nearly as much as I should have. Scarred from my F, I managed a "W" in my electrical engineering class. This was prime evidence I still had much to learn. "W" is a "Withdrawal" -- you probably didn't know you could get those. I dropped the class the day of the deadline to avoid taking the exam for which I would have been totally unable to pass. It was the most complicated math class in engineering. Even worse, the classes were held at 8 a.m. and I was not a morning person. I made a grand total of three lectures to that class.

That wasn't unusual, however, I did usually make at least one class per week. I had an image to uphold with my classmates whom, at this point, didn't even know I was still registered at the school. I just kept hanging out in the homeroom, playing foosball and cards, and then would miraculously show up to write exams. Bill Gates, Steve Jobs and Michael Dell all dropped out and created billion dollar companies (without which I would not have the ability to do what I am doing at this exact moment--writing a book in Word, on my Dell laptop, while connected to the internet through my iPhone.)

The only occasion in which I did make it to every class was when I repeated the same class the next year. I listened to the professor, watched him do the examples, and learned how to solve the problems without doing the exercises. I was a visual and auditory learner who had believed—incorrectly—that I was a book learner. Whoa, wouldn't that have been nice to know in first year?

By far, the smartest person I went to school with was dyslexic and couldn't read the textbooks. He, in turn, had a study mate who didn't understand the course work. She read him the textbook and then he taught her how to do the problems. Learning style. Very important and when not catered to can lead to ridiculous behavior. For mine, I needed to go to class but class was too slow, and I got bored. That was that.

During my MBA coursework, I learned about a trick to keep your mind active. We had all sorts of gum, squishy balls, and things you could "play with" to stimulate your mind while you sat through lecture. It was an amazing trick. Ergo, for all of you kids out there to whom my engineering school performance sounds familiar (all three of you), get a stress ball and squeeze it while you sit in class. I am hopeful that this will prevent you from having a recurring dream that some administrator somewhere investigates your engineering school course work and discovers that you probably shouldn't have earned your degree and invites you back to redo some of your courses. To be clear, no one has done that to me, yet, and it certainly doesn't stop my nightmares.

The best part of University for me (and the reason that I am neither a doctor nor a lawyer despite the fact that I was in college for six years) was because between my third and fourth years, one could elect to do a 16-month work term and actually work in the industry of one's degree. It is the greatest program. Employers get cheap and keen labor and, in return for the labor, the student received experience so that when he or she did go for a full-time job, they were not impacted by the statement "You don't have any experience."

I absolutely LOVED working. It was what I was born to do. School, which had served only as a means to getting into industry, was barely tolerable as it was. After sixteen months of working, I couldn't take it. Now, acting out took on a whole new level and I was considering dropping out to work, thinking I might go back and finish my degree later. That is a funny story. It absolutely would not have happened.

Fortunately, I did go back, but it led to two of my worst "acting out", if you can believe it. Having been asked about my GPA when I got hired for my internship, I decided the marks would matter once I was back at school. So, while I still didn't go to class very often, I did study. It was no longer acceptable to put in no effort and get bad marks.

However, a few arguments with professors ensued:

Exam Question: If the area of a reservoir is 42.03 square miles with a height of 37.4 feet and a porosity of 12.35% and is an undersaturated reservoir with a formation volume factor of 1.353 at 4,000 psi, what is the recoverable volume in place using the 5 analog fields recovery factors. **My answer** 600 million barrels.

I didn't even calculate it with a calculator. I rounded the numbers in my head and wrote down an answer. Next.

I got the question wrong. The answer was 600,011,062.10 million barrels. Seriously, this is a true story.

I went to talk to the professor and said "Um, professor, I think I got the answer right. 600 million barrels." He said "No, you were close. You didn't get the answer."

"Are you serious?!? You must be kidding me. Every single one of those variables is an unknown. Nobody knows the true numbers in the real world. And using analogies? Are you smoking dope? It's a guess. If I had said 500 million barrels, I would probably be close enough."

He, unfortunately, didn't understand things the same way (perhaps this is why I am not a university professor?). I knew what the answer was, I knew how to calculate it, I just chose not to....

By far, my worst offense, or at least in the eyes of the professor who called me out in front of the entire class, was when I questioned a guest lecturer about the content of their thesis, and apparently, quite offensively. In my opinion, it was in no way odious. I was simply engaging in a stimulating debate and asked what I thought was a benign question. To be honest, I don't even remember what the question was. It was sort of "You said in your introduction you would address "X", and I really didn't feel like you addressed it. What do you think about "X"? I showed up for the lecture because of "X", I remember that. The speaker was awful, a Masters' student, apparently, who was presenting their thesis in advance of their defense and the professor had them as their understudy, or whatever you call them. The lecture was a total disappointment, and therefore I posed the question. The politics of doing so had never entered my mind.

The next day, I again triumphantly made it to class since the professor was showing a video that was part of the class content for which you had to be present and couldn't watch at another time and required a paper to be written as part of the final exam. Before starting the video, the professor actually said, "Before we begin, I have to raise an issue." He pointed at me and said "Son, I don't know who you are and I certainly don't know who you *think* you are by asking a question like that yesterday. I was so offended. It's not easy to speak in front of a class of people like you." In front of about 200 people he did this. To me! A call out! Bad idea. I couldn't believe it. There were a few gasps and a few laughs.

I stood up and walked to the end of the aisle and started walking towards him "I said, pick a topic, how long do I have?"

No laughter. The gasps were palpable.

He invited me out of his class, (i.e. as in "Don't come back, ever.") Fortunately, I did get to take the exam, got a B which was my worst mark in fourth year, and graduated.

Obviously, I had a problem with authority. I also had a problem with ego. And I had a problem with everybody else. But, as I reflect on these truly shocking stories (I mean, wow, I can't believe I did that.... I better stop dredging up the past.... What the heck else will I find that I did?), I was the problem for a lot of people. I wasn't a fit for University--not because I couldn't do it--but because it wasn't what inspired me to do my best. Not being inspired is the first sign of not fitting.

It's fortunate for me that a substantial part of our fourth-year engineering curriculum was a team project. As many do when they are younger, like in the school yard as five-year olds, many of the other teams pre-selected their teammates and spent time working on concepts over the summer. And for the four of my team members, when the teacher said, "Find your team!" we looked around and saw everyone was reaching out to each other and grasping at each other's hands as if this were an exercise of life or death. We looked around, no one reaching for us and said, "What do you say, want to be a team?"

Our team, affectionately referred to by its members as the "A" Team, was dissimilar in virtually every way from our other classmates. We had all been in the internship program; had all worked for the last 16 months; and quite frankly were ready for the next challenge. As a result, most of our team meetings involved time at the bar; time playing foosball and irritating the other teams by our total lack of stress with respect to the school year. Whether on purpose or by accident, we didn't even start the project until about the last week of the first semester- we were busy having fun. We were four guys who had been classmates for three years, some closer friends than others, and we were sort of the left-over misfits. It turns out it was the best composition of a team I had ever been on and there was no magic to it. We had a common interest (graduating), a common goal (finishing the project), had complimentary skill sets (or rather didn't compete to do someone else's job- it was expected they would complete it on time and up to standard) and we liked each other. That was it; that was the big mystery. We liked each other and because of that, we didn't want to let each other down.

Perhaps I am too one-sided in my recollection of University, but I do know that my fourth-year project team was the highlight and of everyone I went to school with, they are the only three I say in touch with.

It's interesting to me now, as I reflect on it, that there are many truly successful people (myself, to date, notably excluded from this list) who didn't finish University; some of them didn't even start it! Ultimately, I think University improves your odds at success but passion for what one does and belief in oneself is probably more important. It is a shame that University is considered a rite of passage still to this day when many of the world's most influential business leaders never finished their degrees. What's worse are those people who do receive their degrees and then look down on those that don't. Here's what I think: There are jobs for which you absolutely need a degree. Being a doctor, designing bridges or process equipment, building airplanes. But for most, you need energy, you need desire, and you need opportunity. Some of the smartest people with whom I have ever worked don't have degrees. They have been held back from what they could attain otherwise, and I think it's silly, considering the way I treated my days in University.

My advice on the subject, as you meet and interview people to join your team, don't mistake a *degree* for skill, and don't mistake poor performance for lack of skill; they could truly be in the wrong environment.

Chapter Three

The Oil and Gas Industry: A Short Course

[I debated cutting this chapter but ultimately decided that as a snapshot for how the industry was at the time that I wrote this and how quickly things can change, it provides a good historical perspective to the state of the industry today. Equally importantly, for those reading this outside the oil and gas industry, I believe providing some context to what we do and how we do it is important.]

I believe the oil and gas industry is a fantastic place to work and I feel very fortunate to have been employed in the industry over my entire career. Did you know that, particularly in the last few years, it has been one of the fastest growing industries for employment? This holds true even during a time when the economy has been rather weak. From the beginning of 2007 to 2012, employment in the oil and gas industry jumped by 40% to 162,000 jobs while support positions grew by 35.6% to 286,000 people. During that same time period, the private sector as a whole grew just 1%.[1] (Wow, real research, David – you shouldn't have. No, really, you shouldn't.)

The oil and gas industry is dynamic. It's incredibly challenging, and, like it or not, it creates a product that consumers really want. Amazingly, it does not capture the imagination the way software and finance do. Everyone recognizes the names Bill Gates, Steve Jobs, and Jamie Dimon. But few in the general public, if any, know Rex Tillerson, Jim Hackett, or Harold Hamm. Facebook is more famous than Continental Resources even though both CEOs are billionaires and one creates a product we *really* need. And no, I am not pillaging the Earth or ruining it for future generations. At least no more so than any other industry.

I had an interesting chat with my plumber today and it brought up a larger point about the industry. He asked me if the price of gas and the world's dependence on oil was because energy companies were greedy. It's a fair question and rarely does the media, movies, or other information we see out there answer that simple question. Since a lot of the book is based on my experiences in the industry of choice, I am making the leap that the learnings are applicable in other industries. Therefore, I think it's probably worth presenting some background on the oil and gas industry first.

The oil and gas industry isn't sexy. It isn't featured on many television shows, Dallas notwithstanding, and unless I have been hanging out with the wrong crowd for the last fifteen years, I don't get to have sex with everyone I know and steal money from the family.

The exposure to the oil and gas industry that we do see is in movies like *There will be Blood*, *Promised Land*, *Gasland* and *SpOILed*.

---

[1] U.S. Labor department statistics. http://www.foxbusiness.com/industries/2013/08/08/shale-boom-spurs-rapid-job-growth/

Similar to everything else, entertainment is a huge part of the equation and there are two sides to every story, even funny ones. There is a ton of bias in the media. They only report on so-called "good" stories which are usually about bad things, and we only remember the things that we want to. I get it. I'm sure I only notice the bad press because I'm sensitive to it and I ignore bad press when it is about other industries.

Nonetheless, I think the oil and gas industry is plagued by a lot more misinformation and negativity than others. And while I am biased in my views, I freely and openly acknowledge it so that you can take that into consideration as you read.

Let's start with the products we create. Oil and natural gas. I say natural gas because it is literally a gas, like oxygen. The gas that goes in cars is actually refined oil. The byproduct of that process makes asphalt, on which we drive, among other things.

Oil and gas are the lifeblood of Western civilization. I don't say this lightly. Transportation, and therefore our ability to live in big, affordable houses in the suburbs and fly across the country to see family, depends on it. Petrochemicals, pharmaceuticals, fertilizers, electricity, heating and air conditioning….you catch my drift. It's important.

Oil and natural gas are commodities, so they are traded as a global commodity, and as important costs of living, are frequently reported on. Like gold. Only unlike gold, oil and gas are consumed whereas gold is stored. Every ounce of gold ever made still exists. The same can be said for most precious gems, perhaps with the exception of diamonds which can be used on oil rig drill bits to help drill faster.

In the 70's, OPEC, or the Organization of the Petroleum Exporting Countries, was accused of price coordination. In reality, it was really supply control and there was truth to the accusation. In 2012, OPEC produced 33 million barrels a day of oil production out of the 85 million barrels a day that is produced (one thousand barrels a second.) That's a high percentage but the countries that are members of OPEC are Algeria, Angola, Ecuador, Iran, Iraq, Kuwait, Libya, Nigeria, Qatar, Saudi Arabia, the United Arab Emirates and Venezuela.[2] I have no idea what the "highest quality of life ranking" is, nor how they calculate it, but those countries are 81st, unranked, 52nd, 88th, unranked, 70th, 108th, 41st, 72nd, 69th and 59th, respectively.[3] For reference, Canada is 14, the United States is 13th, Sweden is 5th, and Ireland is ranked number 1st.

As these OPEC countries can hardly govern themselves, I would make the case that their "control" over the oil market is tenuous at best. They set production quotas, countries cheat to increase their revenue, then they over-provide supply and demand stays the same while the price falls.

There's an entire MBA course devoted to supply-demand economics. Consider, if you will, the intersection of the supply curve (S) and the demand curve (Q) when relative to price (P) and quantity (Q). It makes sense, right? As price goes up, you make more (supply.) As price goes down, you buy (demand) more.

---

[2] http://en.wikipedia.org/wiki/OPEC
[3] http://en.wikipedia.org/wiki/Quality-of-life_Index

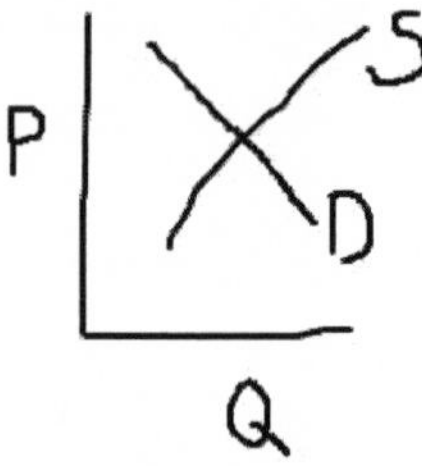

One of my favorite MBA stories, and a big reason I think the person matters more than the degree they have, was about the supply demand curve. It is one of the most important parts of course, and the professor would scribble it on the board, like this:

Just before the final exam, a student came to her and asked "Why do you keep writing 'Lx' on the board? I don't know what that is."

In any event, the politicization of the oil industry is driven by the dependencies our lives have on it--a lot of the wealth of the top 15 countries goes to OPEC to buy oil. Without oil, most of the OPEC countries would have no revenue and would destabilize, negatively impacting the global economy. This isn't a judgment call or an opinion, it is a fact.

ExxonMobil, one of the world's largest producers of the commodity, held the largest market capitalization company on Earth for a long time before Apple took over that spot. I love

Apple and use their products every day, but in terms of importance to the world, there is no comparison. Without the energy industry, nothing else is possible.

In the same context, Apple, which I'm told from their commercials, is the most commonly used camera, music player, and video recorder in the world. They charge $1000 dollars up-front for a nice-looking iPhone X, along with a 2-year cell subscription to use it at ~$100/month. So, you're ultimately in for at least $3,400 for a gadget that costs *maybe* $370 to make in China and uses in-place cellular towers.

Apple doesn't get accused of price fixing. Verizon doesn't get accused of price fixing. Yet, ExxonMobil, who controls less than 3% (roughly 2.5 million barrels) of the world's daily oil production per day, does. Three percent is not much, and it certainly cannot influence the price of the commodity.

I am sorry that gasoline costs so much and that over recent years it has been getting more expensive. As we drill in more and more challenging environments, into deeper and deeper reservoirs, the costs to develop oil and natural gas go up. As costs go up and demand goes up, supply must keep pace and therefore prices, too, must also go up to ensure there is enough supply.

***

The energy industry--like most industries--has had its share of black eyes environmentally, namely, the Exxon Valdez and BP Macondo. Not good. It is truly unfortunate from every aspect, no one in the industry is proud of it, and we all strive every day to do better. The operators pay the billions it costs to clean it up, they pay the massive fines associated with it, and they work to restore the economies of the regions and do everything in their power to restore the region to its previous state.

Now, someone might say "The fines are small in comparison." To what? Like every industry, the goal is to produce a profit. Spills result in having a loss of product, a loss of profit, and cause damage far beyond the cost of a fine. BP lost $70 billion in market value because of the Macondo incident. It became financially strapped, undervalued, and constantly in the penalty box. It hasn't bought any assets of late and has been a frequent divestor, handing control of the assets to other companies. The entire company is dying a slow and painful death, and is now a fertile stalking ground for the other companies in the industry to pick over its carcass and take their great assets make them better and produce more energy for the world in a safer, more economic, and more beneficial way. It is the circle of business. Maybe Scott was right. Some companies should just die.

However, in terms of environmental disasters, other industries haven't fared much better. Testing the nuclear bomb in the desert and over the ocean would have to be among some of the top offenses. Dumping trash into the sea. Chemicals into rivers. The mine in Butte, Montana.

Where is society's culpability? What the F@&k is Wrong with Everybody Else? Us. Collectively.

We--society--make choices as to what things should cost. Just as we accept the iPhone's cost, we think oil is too expensive.

Did you know that there are 42 gallons in a barrel? A barrel of milk costs $168 and it is renewable. Gatorade costs about $560 a barrel and it's basically sugar and water. For goodness sake, Dasani water costs about $560 a barrel and it's just water.

Oil costs what it costs because governments don't tax it as highly as they should. Namely, because it's unpopular with voters and because it's use is so widespread and essential, it hurts lower classes disproportionately.

And so, we talk about the renewables. Solar. Wind. Very expensive. It's sunny at best 75% of the day and it's not always windy.

Nuclear plants haven't been approved in the United States for decades and with the threat of terrorism higher now than at any point in the past, I have a hard time seeing this change anytime soon.

Coal. Coal employs a lot of people in swing states. There are lots of power companies in the United States and, equally importantly, trains have to ship coal and generate huge profits. These industries are unionized and have amassed many high paying jobs from lots of voters. And yet in terms of efficiency, coal pollutes more and creates less energy than does natural gas.

So, society continues to attack the oil and gas industry, which isn't generally unionized because the Rockefellers fought it, as WalMart does today. Much of the oil production we consume in the U.S. is foreign [*this is still true though production has increased dramatically as a result of the Permian, at the end of 2019 we are at "Peak U.S. Oil production' and it will be true again soon enough*], so it is an easy rally cry because we don't generate taxes or royalties on oil. The car industry on the other hand, which is unionized, domestic, and an employer of many people in swing states like Michigan, realizes that if oil was not consumed through gasoline, it would then be left with millions upon millions of used cars that have outdated technology. Resale values would be destroyed, companies would fail and ultimately, the consumer would be pushed to a product that it isn't willing to pay up for. Electric cars are more expensive to buy, even subsidized, and regardless of the consumer telling everyone who would listen that they love the environment; they drive their gas guzzling cars. My point here is that the politics of the situation, not the realities of it, dictate media and government response. For ethanol, which is blended with gasoline to make it more environmentally friendly, sugarcane from Brazil is the most environmentally friendly product to make it with a very small carbon footprint and yet the U.S. government who says it wants to reduce our carbon footprint puts tariffs on importing ethanol from sugarcane so that corn-based ethanol produced in the U.S. (much less efficiently) gets a higher price and subsidizes the farmers that make it, as well as pushing up food prices around the world due to increased demand (and therefore price) for corn.

All that being said, the oil and gas industry still has a long way to go. Spills will sometimes be a regrettable by-product of production. Fortunately, however, most are extremely small volumes and have minimal environmental impact. Nevertheless, we must be vigilant every day and focus on safety and the environment as the number one concern. We have a social license to operate and we must do our absolute utmost to put the environment, our stakeholders and our employees.

This is not just an idle statement. For example, North Dakota is absolutely booming right now. It has the most abundant oil field in the U.S. and it's exploding. Unemployment is less than 3.5%--even less, really, because anyone who wants to work can. Wages are skyrocketing, there are no places to live, hotels are extremely expensive, and it is making many farmers, local businesspeople, and U.S. businesses that operate there very rich.

Recently, I had to go to North Dakota for a meeting that was scheduled after my family and I left from Colorado, traveled through North Dakota for the meeting, and then on to Calgary.

I am not a protective husband. In fact, my wife is a much better driver than am I. One morning, my field superintendent picked me up at 6 a.m. to go to the meeting and the plan was that I would meet my family about six hours later. An audible was quickly called on that plan and I backtracked two hours solely to pick my wife and the kids up because she hadn't had field driver training. It only takes one misstep among the trucks carrying oil, pipe, and parts before a car meets its end. And with an overworked, extremely stretched workforce, alertness behind the wheel is absolutely essential. I had always believed it, but on that trip, I became fanatical about it--safety and getting people home to their families--is the most important thing we ever do.

You only die once, but your family dies every anniversary, birthday and Christmas thereafter. Be safe.

While we are on the subject of dying, let's talk about fracture stimulation. To hear about it in the news today, it's an epidemic.... In reality, it's not, but that's why we watch the news, to be horrified about the most benign things. Fracture stimulation on a well, better known as a frac (not with a k.... only people who don't know what they are talking about spell it with a k.) Frac'ing is the reason that wells in North America produce. Fluid is pumped at high rates and pressures into the reservoir that holds the oil and the gas. All this takes place miles below the surface and the oil and gas literally exists in rock (not in "pools" as some might imagine). It is stored in between the grains of sand that have long since turned to rock. To help you picture it, imagine a beach. Now pile millions of years of sediment on that beach and add heat. It turns to rock. All of the rock was on the surface at some point. It's bewildering to imagine the churning of the earth's surface, the movement of oceans, of rivers, and of sediment all created these precious commodities. And it's equally beguiling to see geologists who interpret these fantastical events and identify where prospective reservoirs of oil and gas are.

The organic material that was buried in generally the same period of time, within millions of years anyway, is called the source. This source, usually a swamp with lots of plants and fish and dinosaurs (kidding, it's mostly plants) gets buried, and as it's heated, it turns that organic material to oil. Add more heat as the rock gets buried deeper and over longer periods of time, it gets super-cooked and turns purely to gas. Since oil is lighter than water and gas lighter than both, the oil and gas start to migrate in the rock. They finally stop migrating when they find "seals", which are bits of rock with no ability for fluid to flow through it. The oil and gas get trapped and remain there indefinitely. Then one day, an oil company takes a lease from a farmer or the state or the federal government, drills a well, pays a fee to the owner of the minerals and Tada!, you have oil and gas production.

As the years have gone by, the rock in which oil and gas is found has gotten poorer, harder to exploit, and deeper to drill and the only way to produce oil and gas from these formations is to frac them. Without frac'ing, energy production would go on terminal decline in this county. Simply put, frac'ing is required in order to produce energy in North America. It is safe. It is necessary. It provides an essential resource. Driving would become extremely expensive; heating our homes would be tough; we would import even more oil and more North American wealth would find its way to countries that have looser environmental regulations, and in which are easier to drill. It's that simple. We make choices.

We make tradeoffs. Until we have alternatives that are cost equivalent without subsidy, we will use fossil fuels, or we will pay more. Choices.

To the question of "Do oil companies prevent conversion from oil to alternate energy as a result of profit motive?". I submit that most energy companies would benefit if the world, en masse, converted to electric and compressed natural gas (CNG) cars. CNG is more environmentally friendly when the electricity is made from natural gas, not coal. CNG is an abundant, land-locked resource that would reduce our demand in oil and all the energy companies that operate in places like Angola and Iraq would be able to produce natural gas at better prices (because demand would go up, supply would lag and prices would increase) in more politically friendly environments. That would be far preferable.

And, a last note looking to the future and speaking of 'environmentally friendly cars', I can say that I think the Tesla is pretty fantastic having just ridden in one for the first time last week. Fully electric, very few moving parts, a tremendous amount of storage, an unbelievable amount of acceleration with no gear shifts, and no sound whatsoever. It has redefined cars as we know them and will shift consumption patterns because it truly is the greatest car I have ever been in. It will destroy the auto union in the United States because there are no retiree benefits built into the price of the car, no dealership fees, very little inventory on backorder, and it is a superior and disruptive technology. It's similar to what Apple did with its iPhone to RIM's Blackberry and could easily bankrupt the remaining auto companies. In doing so, it could bring in an age that leads to the necessary infrastructure investments required to move away from oil in its entirety.

[Yeah, I wrote that. As you know, I spend much of my time in 2019 speaking of the disconnect between 'patterns of consumption' vs. blaming climate change on fossil fuels. It is important to remember that 27% of electricity produced in the United States comes from coal and that 35% comes from natural gas. Forgetting where lithium batteries come from and the environmental impact to mine lithium, consumers must remember that 20 million barrels of crude oil are consumed in the United States each day. 70% of this is used in transportation. So, while electric vehicles are wonderful, we will need a lot more coal and natural gas electric generation to provide the power needed to fuel 20 million barrels a day worth of energy. But that is a much larger topic and one for another book entirely.

***

There is a book called "The myth of the ethical consumer" by Gianna Eckart. I haven't read it but I heard her on a podcast and let's be honest, the title tells you everything you need to know.

Consumers can hate where a product comes from or how it is made and still buy it. The only way behavior changes is to legislate it out. And on the topic of legislation- let's get real about carbon emissions: if we want to reduce them, consumers MUST pay more.

Here's a fun stat. The U.S. uses 9.33 million barrels of oil for gasoline each day and a 0.25/gallon gas tax would reduce it to 9.23 million (that's not a lot).

Here's another stat: ride sharing services have increased total miles driven in cities by 160%. The problem of reducing emissions is easy: dramatically raise gasoline taxes and tell consumers (voters) we are saving the planet. Now which politician is brave enough to actually tell the truth??

#hottakeoftheday, February 24, 2019

Chapter Four

Big Companies

When I started my career, my dad and I talked at least seven times a day. He was my advisor, had so much to tell me, and I just loved talking to him. We were the same people and I wanted to be exactly like him when I grew up. He "retired" from a big company for what I can only imagine were many of the same traits that I exhibited early in my career.

And like him, I had my mom to try to set me straight. Such was my upbringing with one parent an oil and gas executive and the other a teacher, then principal, then, when my dad retired, the head of a large nonprofit in Calgary that did amazing things in the community and made her one of the more respected leaders in that great city.

Nonetheless, dad's traits were my natural inclinations and mom wasn't always there (though she tried!). In the mirror, at least in my mirror, we were big company men who needed big company assets with a big company budget. Also, in said mirror, we were pioneers--breaking boundaries and injecting thinking that was going to transform the big companies into greater, bigger companies that everyone loved to work for. Really, at twenty-two, I thought like this.

It was my blind and unwavering belief that big companies defined career success. I used to hear people say that about themselves; that they had started some business and how freeing it was that they worked for themselves. It sounded awful to me. It sounded limited to me. Why would you want to work for yourself when you could run Apple or…. just somewhere important?

It took me fifteen years to discover that big companies aren't the "be all, end all." They are great places to start, to learn, to grow, and to see if you can survive the culture long enough to run it. And for those who can make it there over your entire career, I congratulate you. You have done very well, made a very nice living, and have a comfortable retirement ahead of you. Additionally, I apologize for all the jokes that we--those who couldn't last--make about the lobotomy scars. They add character, in my opinion.

I promise I won't be mean. I promise I won't be mean. I promise I won't be mean.

I have lots of stories about big companies, as does everyone. One of my favorites is a Mobil story, pre-Exxon. Mobil had purchased a company and for anti-trust reasons, had to keep it separate for two years. They staffed it with smart, capable people and went about their way to pass the two years. At the end of the two years, they folded the company into Mobil and shut down the division.

My friend, from whom the story comes, moved on to a new company and was surprised when two years later, Mobil started buying land in the play that they had been working on and had subsequently mothballed.

It turned out that the approval for the project had been given and the train had left the station. Someone in some part of the company unknown had an order to buy the land as soon as it became available--which it did, two years later without the team to staff it and long after the play had been deemed no longer worth pursuing.

But they are big, they are powerful, they have unlimited opportunities for smart people and, for a long time, they were *it* for me.

Now, I admit, most people are probably a lot smarter about these sorts of things than I was; they probably didn't obsess about their careers and their progression and their future, and so I realize what I am about to say is obvious to most of you: Big companies are not the pinnacle.

For the seven of you that read that and were glad you were seated, this book is for you. For the rest of you, you can be amused that it took me all of fifteen years to figure that out. Big companies are <u>one</u> option amongst a myriad of possibilities. Big companies were built by somebody, and that somebody probably worked for someone at some time, and thought to themselves, "Why am I working for this jackass when I could be working for myself?"

I firmly believe that, as a decision, working for a big company at the onset of your career is the best decision you can make--even if you are like me. You get great training, you get to work for a lot of people, and you get to see how people interact. Top performers, middle performers and bottom performers--all the way up and down the chain.

You make decisions on how you want to manage or work, and probably equally important, how you don't want to manage and work.

No matter where you think you may end up in your career, the best time to work for a big company is at the onset. When you are young and smart and working for someone else, usually in a big company, uniqueness means you have potential. But the objective is to train out the unique and keep the potential. You make gaffes, but they are the mistakes of the young; they are forgiven. Demanding people be fired in the hallway, for example, while frowned upon, is not career-limiting if you have potential.

As you age, and don't become less unique as intended, this uniqueness is no longer cute or naïve. Deciding, for example, that a monthly asset review was a waste of your team's time and therefore not spending the three days getting ready every month to answer every minor question was a unique problem. And when your uniqueness becomes a problem, you no longer have potential. The first time, I left. The second time, I got fired. I was a slow learner, apparently.

Since in my mind's eye I wasn't aware that there was anything other than "big" companies, I tried to force fitting in. I fought performance systems, everything was a hill, and I wanted to create the company into what *I* wanted it to be.

As time went by and I fought more and more for what I believed in, as work consumed more and more of me, I started to become an asshole. Not to those that I needed at work. That was never my style, management or otherwise. I was not the slave-driving, fear-mongering boss. My door was always open; I had time for everyone and their problems; we were a team; we were a family; and together, we could do anything. OK, the As, some Bs and me could do anything- like I said, not good with Cs.

Funny, I wasn't anything like that at home. At home, I would vent. I couldn't make any of the changes I promised; I knew how to implement all the solutions that could fix what was causing everyone problems. Why wouldn't they just get out of my way and let me fix it?

I used to be fun. And funny. And silly. And most importantly, I didn't take myself seriously. And then, one day, I wasn't any of those things. It was a slow march. I didn't even know it was happening.

How does the same person go from fun-loving to asshole? In my opinion, two words. Culture and fit.

Have you ever been in a straitjacket or locked in a small room? The more experience I got, the more confident I became, and the more I saw, the more I was being restricted by what I was allowed to be, not what I was. The harder I tried to conform, the more I found myself carrying everyone. I don't think that it's because they didn't believe in what we were trying to do, they just didn't understand why I was trying to do it.

Eventually, I was the only one solving and I was getting angry with people. And when you get angry with people, you lose perspective, you lose sanity and eventually, you lose your job.

What advice can I give about perspective, now that I have some?

No career is worth the pain. If you are struggling every day to get through it, you dislike your coworkers, you dislike your boss and find yourself drinking more, exercising less, or snapping at family, you aren't in the right place. I'm not saying you need to go start a business or quit every three months and be irresponsible just because you had a bad day. But I can tell you as someone who was there, find something else and find it sooner than later.

I've been out of work now for eighteen months. Don't interpret this to mean that I don't earn money. What I do to make money is my hobby--I get to help people start businesses, find solutions to problems, and make their own companies more successful. When the day is done, I write; I coach hockey; I play golf; I drink wine. Most importantly, my bad days aren't that bad, and my good days are phenomenal. I promise you that you can have that too, so go and get it. Maybe if I went back to a "real" company and a "real" job, I would find that what I lacked was balance in my life. Perhaps. But I believe that I wasn't doing what I loved and how I loved to do it, and, as a result, I wasn't able to be balanced. Being happy allowed me that chance.

You have more power than you think. When I was "The Boss", our leadership team had discussions every year around performance review time. We had less than eighty staff and we had a habit of taking two full days and talking about every single person in the company. What they made, what they did, how they performed, and where they were going in their careers. I knew what everybody made, what everybody's bonuses and raises were, and their all-important performance ratings. What did I learn from it?

I learned that if you are good, you can set the terms. And if you aim for a win–win deal, you will likely get it. And if you don't get it, you will be free and clear and have no qualms about finding your place in the world that will allow you to be much happier and better appreciated.

Culture Doesn't Change. Oh, how I wanted this one not to be true. I tried extremely hard. I fired people, I had group bonding, team building, inclusive meetings, exclusive meetings, internal meetings, coaching, training and everything in between. Culture is the sum of the people who are there at the time you are there. It will not change until they are gone. And there are some people that will never leave. And so, you have to fire them, and I have learned that when you fire people, it's not the people that you fire that are the problem, it's their friends. It's who is left behind, and the way they band together to prevent the change that you are trying to make.

I don't want to confuse you here. I started the book talking about how being fired was awful. And yet, it was the right thing. However, there is a right way to do it. There is a respectful and decent way to treat people. But this book isn't about sunshine and unicorns and ice cream. It's about the real world, and sometimes people have to go.

Nonetheless, in most cases, you can't get rid of enough people to start to change the culture, and by the time you have dispersed enough people, you have created a lot of baggage, a lot of enemies, and there is a high probability that you, too, will be fired, as I was.

So, when that person sits at the desk, talking for hours, not doing their work, your company has made the decision that it is the cost of doing business and that the cost of addressing this issue, in changing the culture, is too high. Don't lament. Either accept it or move on. Or refer to my previous lesson in which you have more power than you think. Ask for what you need and if you don't get it, don't hope for change. Hope is not a plan. Pack your stuff, grab the goldfish and head to the door, hopefully with more than just a mission statement.

It's about people. The more friends you have at work, the happier you will be. When everyone in the workplace is different from you, you aren't going to fit in. You aren't going to have fun. You aren't going to be happy. And since you spend most of your adult awake life at work, or at home thinking about work, if you don't connect with the people you work with, you aren't going to find long-term happiness. The only thing I miss now are the people I have worked with and with whom I had so much fun solving problems. The only reason I want to grow my hobby into something bigger is so that I can get that back. Because I honestly believe that similar-minded people who like and respect and trust each other can create something so much beyond what any one person could create It's a thesis I want to prove.

You are always living the dream That it isn't necessarily your dream isn't the point. No matter how much your job and life sucks, I want you to think about this: Somewhere, at this very moment, you are living the dream of an 8-year-old carpet weaver in a third world country.

Chapter Five

Being Fired: What I Learned

In the days, weeks and now years since "The Event", I have reflected on the question "What have I learned?" a lot. That which doesn't kill you makes you stronger, apparently.

This past fall, I received an email from a college friend I that hadn't talked to in more than five years and with whom I was on the fourth-year project team in engineering together. Apparently, I had dropped off the face of the Earth, Facebook, LinkedIn and Twitter news notwithstanding, and he was just checking in. We exchanged the typical catch up details- him going first- and I reflected, with satisfaction, at how much things have changed for me since I got fired and how they have truly changed for the better. Anna, the HR person at BakkenCo before Phillis, read a draft of the book and suggested my target market should be outplacement agencies; she also contemplated quite openly about what advice she could have given me in the year before I got fired that could have made things different for me. She recognized even then my personality, my drive, my "everything" wasn't a fit for BakkenCo, but she didn't know how to say it.

For Jarrett, my college friend, he wasn't surprised that I got fired: his observation on the matter was "I always wondered when you would push your boundaries enough at some point to outgrow any company you worked for." Interesting. A guy I haven't seen in fifteen years and hadn't talked to for five knew what would happen to me long before I did. It seems the big secret was that everybody knew it but me.

I had a very high-flying career; I had moved up very fast in all the organizations I had been a part of, and I had designs on running one day. A big one; an important one; it was to be the pinnacle of my achievement and reflection of my contributions. This abstract concept kept me focused; helped me work through my daily frustrations and ensured I would work through every challenge presented. What this concept prevented was the self-awareness that maybe my goals and my anticipated career path, did not fit with my personality. My college buddy knew it. Anna knew it. It seems everyone who has ever met me knew it. Sadly, it took being fired for me to know it (and even then, it took a long time after).

One of the biggest takeaways I had was that you have more power than you think, and what you think is power can be taken away. I will start with the power being taken away.

That which "defined" me was taken away and what I didn't know then, because I had always been on the delivering end, is that firing is about personal relationships, in my mind, the performance is a mitigating circumstance. I think the evidence in this is that really, if you think about it, very few "poor" performers--those that just come to work and leave quietly without actually working--are fired. I used to see them all the time and they drive me crazy, as I'm sure they do you. And yet when you think back to the people who have been let go, I venture to say very few of them were fired for poor performance; I would venture to say they were fired for fit.

At Anadarko, where I worked for the first ten years of my career, I coined the term "RIP" for "Retired-in-Place" to describe the worst offenders of my sense of equity in the workplace. It's actually a brilliant strategy! You can go for years at the end of your career, talking about retirement every day and what you are going to do when you retire (that's the diversion, implying that you aren't really retired!), collecting your pension (known to others as their salary), until management finally deals with you. And in the jackpot scenario, the company gives you a package just for you to leave. God forbid you contact a lawyer! But I digress. And Anadarko was a pretty assertive a "pay for performance" company for the most part.

I promise I won't be mean again. I promise I won't be mean again. I promise I won't be mean again.

Companies *like* to say "pay for performance." I apologize if I am offending you when I say in my fifteen years, I have never encountered a true "pay for performance" company nor have I talked to anyone that works for this mythical beast. It's very easy to say "pay for performance," but I've been in the room talking about raises and promotions at a company that believed they were "pay for performance" company and what I saw was that the difference in raises between our absolute best performers and our absolute worst usually was 0% - 4%. Wow. In many cases, the salary differences were 30-40% which, in the absolute dollar sense, often a poor performer got a larger monetary raise than the top performer. A true "pay for performance" culture probably doesn't have HR people in the room moderating these discussions and top performers would rarely switch jobs for a 15% raise, as they often need to do to get their salary on par with their contribution.

There is a huge distinction between performance in the business world and performance in the sports world. In the sports world, performance is judged on tangible results that are easy to see; you win, you score, you excel. The high value people get rewarded regardless of their "experience" level and they also get treated differently: more playing time, more time with the press, more leeway if things aren't going so well. In sports, the low value people get cut even if they used to be high valued players. Perform or die; a meritocracy. And no HR people. One of my MBA classmates, Brad, used to play for the Los Angeles Kings. After the lockout in 2004/2005, his agent asked him about his plans. Brad said that he was looking forward to the hockey season. His agent said, "You know what, Brad. You are a great guy, your teammates love you, but you're not that good a hockey player. You should do something with your fame, get your MBA and get a job." Brad wasn't upset. Brad didn't get self-righteous. Brad agreed and that's why he was my MBA drinking buddy. Business--and particularly big business--does not work this way. More importantly, it will never work this way. Before I was fired, I didn't know this. In the business world, performance is more subtle, and ratings are subjective.

In years past, I have described team members in many different ways. I liked to describe my top people as "rock stars" but I had no character foil. A "groupie" implies something entirely different and an "accordion player" was far too subtle for anyone, me included, to understand. I once overheard a manager say to their employee "We have bricks and we have mortar. You are the brick." Huh? What does that even mean? Generally speaking, when you have to explain your reference, it is not a good reference.

The most apt way, I think, is to rank people in an organization as "A" players, "B" players, and "C" players. While some have different definitions and perspectives on what constitutes these categories, my definition is as follows: An "A" player is the driver, the strongest on the team, the workhorse and initiative taker; the "B" player supports the "A" player, knows that they are there to support the "A" player, and they are great at it. They won't light the world on fire, but if you don't have them, you will be sorry. Then there are the "C" players. You don't need "C" players. They take up a lot of management time, they are frustrating to deal with, and it was "C" players with whom I personally had no idea how to interact.

When I started writing this book during the days that followed being fired, low "B" and "C" players were my target--their mediocrity and averageness had consumed me. The "retired in place", the "social coordinators", the "sickies", the "snowies", the "I'm working from homies." They all went to work February 1st. The nearly divorced "Oh yes, please sir, may I have some more, sir?" slaves to the company did not. That the low "B" and "C" players could survive and I be destroyed was confounding. I find that comical now. So, what I learned, lesson number one? Nobody else matters. Everybody else is everybody else's problem. So, don't worry about "them."

The same person can be an "A" to one person and a "B" or even a "C" to someone else. A lot of times, category movement happens when you lose a relationship with someone. And when you lose that relationship, especially when you are a senior person in the organization, the cleanest way is to fire them. No fuss. No mess. No bother. I lost the relationship with my boss, and I assumed that because I was still performing at the level I had always performed and doing the things I had always done, I was still considered an "A" player.

I also thought I was irreplaceable. Everyone is replaceable.

Takeaway 1: Be aware of your place in an organization. You always have a boss, no matter how incredible you are at your job, and they can stop liking you really, really fast. I'm not saying you have to turn off your brain, but if there is friction, you have to be aware of what can come next.

Takeaway 2: If you rock the boat, you don't always get to stay on board, either because the ride is too rough or because the others on the boat don't want you there anymore.

Takeaway 3: Not everyone likes a crisis. If you are someone who thrives on crises, be careful not to be perceived as the creator of the crisis. Whether you were the initiator of said crises or not, if people start seeing you in the middle of every crisis, it becomes less about the issue and more about you.

Takeaway 4: Define yourself by who you are, not what you do. At least in my experience, when I'm at a social event, the two most frequently asked questions are "What do you do?" (if they don't know you) and "How's work?" (if they do know you). It's one step more familiar than "Some crazy weather we've been having…" but similarly frequent.

"Hi, nice to meet you, Sarah. And what do you do?"

"I love yoga and I eat at this unbelievable restaurant once a week. I have two girls; I edit books and I love Starbucks tea."

I pray that one day, someone says exactly that. When I was fired and subsequently unemployed--or at least not employed with a job that was "impressive"—that mere nicety was the most terrifying part of any social interaction and part of what hurt so much in the weeks that followed. I defined myself first by where I worked, then by the role I had, and assigned my confidence based on the answer. I wasn't working for myself; I was working for someone else. And as long as you're not the boss, it can be taken from you.

Since February 1st, 2012, I've spoken with a lot of people who have been fired. I have a theory, and as I've suggested before, was the original theme of the book: Mediocrity was "What's Wrong." Mediocrity is the middle and anyone who has studied statistics knows that the middle of the bell curve is where society lives. It is out on the fringes, in both directions, that one stands out--the truly bad and the truly good. The truly bad get fired, quit, or just figure out a way to survive. The truly good climb until there is no place to go--either no higher or out.

There is no support group; no church basement meeting; but we find each other nonetheless. Some are still deeply bitter and really struggling to come to grips with it.

For most of us, our career was our life. Everything we did and every interaction we had was centered around our careers so when it was gone, it was as though a part of who you were was taken away. But I now believe that you get a part of yourself back--the best part; the part that always stood above the crowd;

the part that rocked the boat and stood above mediocrity-- and you create a place in the world where you belong.

I used to think about it a lot, and I used to be angry about it. The irony was that the company I gave my life for gave it back to me the day I was fired. Whether the intent was "just business" or, as I contend, strictly personal, it turned out to be the most crucial day of my life. More importantly, by taking away the power I thought I had, I discovered the power I did have. With sixteen months of transition and now fully into the next adventure, I smile constantly and can honestly say that being fired is the best thing that has ever happened to me.

Chapter Six

A Journey of Self Discovery

I was in New York earlier this year when I was still trying to sort through starting a business, having a failed business and transitioning between ventures. More on that later but for now, I needed a sentence to explain why I was in New York.

And when I go to New York, my favorite thing to do is walk. I walk everywhere. New York is a city that seems to have a new city every ten blocks--a new vibe, a new ethnic flavor, a new pace. It's truly amazing and it is my favorite city in the U.S.

I know there are a lot of people who don't like New York, but I would encourage them to stay somewhere in midtown (that's about 50th Street to the uninitiated) and walk north through Central Park up to the Museum of Civilization and the Guggenheim, then over to Lexington to walk down through the shops. Next, jump in a cab and head to the Brooklyn Bridge down the FDR with a real NY cabbie; walk across the bridge; take the subway back towards midtown by the Freedom Tower, The Village, Soho and NYU Campus towards Bryant Park. When 4:30 p.m. arrives, hang out by the Public Library as people are finishing their day and carving out a small sliver of solitude from the masses. It's a lot. It takes two whole days. But I promise, at the end of that voyage you will know New York a lot better.

Having done that walk already, one night I ended up in *Hell's Kitchen*--a place that I had never ventured into before and only ended up there because I wanted to see where Jon Stewart broadcasts his show. It was spring, and since I am part Canadian, that equates to hockey playoffs. I needed a bar with a TV. It's New York and fortunately, there is a restaurant in almost every building. But as Murphy's Law portends, when you want one, you can't find one. Although every bar I walked by had a TV, mind you, they were watching things that definitely weren't hockey: bass fishing, women's softball, Duck Dynasty, the Harlem Globetrotters and so on, but no hockey. I was starting to get desperate. My judgment was waning, my pulse quickening, and I had beer on the mind. This is always a bad combination.

Finally! A haven. A sports pub. ***Boxers***. Sweet. I knew it! New York has everything. I relaxed.

I walk in, pull out my ID, and showed the bouncer. He smiles and says, "Have a great time." Okay, I will!

Odd…. he was awfully thin for a New York bouncer.

I'm walking at top pace, as I do when I'm on the move, bee-lining for the bar (which I think adequately describes a straight line). I am about half-way into the bar when I stopped to take stock of the crowd so I can, you know, get a vibe; figure out where to stand; get a lay of the land. There are a lot of guys here. Well it *is* a sports pub. But, I mean, *a lot* of guys.

As I head to the bar, I spot the bartender. I don't so much as "spot" him as I become "aware" of him and the other two bartenders simultaneously. They are all wearing boxing shorts. Only boxing shorts. Aha! As per the name on the front door. ***Boxers.*** No shirts. Makes sense if you are a boxer. Cute gimmick. Wait a second….

So, I had a choice: hightail it back out of the bar or commit. I went with commit. I ordered a beer, slinked off to the corner, and watched my hockey game. After the initial shock wore off, I started to survey my surroundings. When in Rome…. Step 1. I needed a plan as to how I was going to fend off the onslaught of guys wanting my attention.

I mean, what do you say? "I'm not gay?" No. Too obvious. "Sure, I'd like a drink, but I don't go to first base on the first date?" No. Too much of a lie.

As it happened, I didn't need to say anything. No one approached me. "What the F@&K is wrong with everyone? Here I am! Come and get me boys!"

After ten minutes, I found myself starting to try and appeal to people so they would come over and say hi. Eye contact. Running my hands through my hair. Laughing at nothing in particular (since I wasn't talking to anyone.) Nobody came over and I left feeling that even a straight guy is a little bit queer in a gay bar.

***

When I was younger, I played competitive squash to supplement my boredom at school. Or perhaps it was the vice versa? When I started my oil and gas career and gradually had less time to play competitive squash, my boss told me I was "intense" and that "Maybe I should take up painting." Seriously--I can't make this stuff up. So, like Bob Ross, The Happy Painter, I painted four hours a week in class, always muttering under my breath "There, let's add some nice leaves to that tree… Oh, isn't that beautiful." I was a horrible painter. It didn't calm me down, and I continued to not fit in.

Then I went to a smaller company (but still a big company relatively speaking), one where I really thought I could make a positive influence and make it better. I got fired. In truth, it was because I didn't know that there was something out there other than big companies and that, quite simply, I might just not fit in. I misdiagnosed a lot of my personality quirks. I thought they were unique. They were actually symptoms of something far different. My friends and family knew it long before I did, and it took me a long time acknowledge it. And, more importantly, to believe that it was perfectly acceptable.

I'm an entrepreneur.

There, I said it. God, it feels good to say. I suppose it's like being gay, or at least I imagine it's like being gay. All your friends know, most of them don't care, and no one can understand why it took you so long to figure out.

The first time I heard this phrase uttered about me, it hit me like a ton of bricks. I was raising money and describing the way we could take a deal that no one else on earth was willing to buy and break it apart, rebuild it, redefine it, and fix it. He stared at me and simply said: "Wow. An engineer who's an entrepreneur. What a combination."

"What the F@&K are you talking about?" was what instantly raced through my mind. Here I am pouring out my soul, trying to make you an ungodly amount of money and you have to call me that! Unbelievable! I will admit that I am creative; I am non-conformist; I see a solution in every problem; a business plan in every idea; a deal in every discussion; but I am not an entrepreneur. Asshole.

It turns out that he was right. It is quite possible that most of the angst I had in my career, the choices I had made, the companies I had worked for, were because I was unable to see myself for what I really was. So, I have designed a questionnaire that should help you.

Step 1. Find a friend.

Step 2. Ask them: Am I an entrepreneur?

Step 3. Trust their judgment.

I just wish someone had taught me that in business school.

Book 3

What They Didn't Teach You in Business School

A Memoir of Lessons

Book Three, Lesson One

Accept Who You Are

There were never supposed to be three books in this journey. As you know, my advice on losing weight is profound, and I probably should have stopped there. But as you know, I'm all for breaking convention.

This part of the journey, the longest part of the book, is about how the learnings have brought me to where I am. And by where I am, I certainly don't mean it as a how-to guide to anything. I am not a guide. But here we are; me still writing, you still reading, and so I suppose our relationship is working so far. I'll do my best. Learnings so far: Writing books is hard and getting fired is good for you. *If* it only happens once. I can also tell you, I'm happy for the first time in a very, very long time.

During that very long time, I wanted to be …. I don't even know. If I'm honest, and since I'm using all my best jokes and material here, I might as well just put it all out there: I wanted to be what I assumed everyone else thought I should be. Or rather, perhaps, HOW I should be. I'm sure you have felt the same thing on occasion, or every day. And the issue is not living someone else's dream or letting others live vicariously through you; it's being humble enough that you don't know the answers and maybe someone is guiding the way. My experience is that it's like having kids--you can only figure it out by doing it. When I got fired and embarked on a journey with no advice and with lots of mistakes, I finally found a place that worked for me. It isn't a place that will necessarily work for you. But I believe that having awareness and knowing that you can have whatever it is you want can be empowering enough for you to find a place that works for you.

There is an old proverb "Grant me the serenity to accept the things I cannot change, courage to change the things I can, and the wisdom to know the difference." It's a good saying; cute, makes sense, but rarely do we heed the advice.

Are you happy in your job right now?

Do you complain to your co-workers and say things like "If only my boss would do this." or "Why do we do it this way?" or "Why can't we hire someone to help me? I'm so overworked."

Spouses don't change, companies don't change, and cultures don't change. I used to be a visionary boss. Like me or hate me, everyone would say I had vision. I used to believe it was my best quality. I could look out over the horizon, see the world I wanted it to be, and commit to change the world. My team believed in me, and I embarked on a fight to change it.

What I didn't know then but now recognize was that I couldn't change the company and I didn't accept that. I thought through strength of will and of character, the company would bend to my desires and I would create a place where my team, my co-workers, and those that would follow would love to work, be the happiest they had ever been, and never leave.

Accept the things I cannot change.

I talked people out of leaving many times. I always said, "If you are thinking of picking up the phone, come talk to me, we will make it better." For all my good intentions, I couldn't. I tried so hard and even when I talk to friends or family today, my instinct is to fight: Never, ever, ever give up.

The reality is you have a choice. You can accept the company for what it is today; not what you want it to be. Regardless of what your boss wants to do, says he or she can do, or talks about being able to do in six months, the company is what it is. Work within the structure of today and assess "Can I stay here, as-is, and be happy?" If the answer is yes, then I am very happy for you. Contentment at work is actually THE most important thing at work.

If the answer is no, then you must have the courage to change what you can. What you can change is you- or at least the way you are-within the confines of the company. If you want another role or another boss or more flexible work hours or four days a week or a chance to get licensed or take courses paid for by the company- whatever *it* is that will get you to "I can accept everything else at the company and be happy if I do X", then that is what you must do.

Have the courage to change what you can.

There is a big culture clash between the baby boomers and generation Y apparently. I see it in the news all the time and I hear both generations above and below me complain about it. Talent is a scarce resource and climbing the ladder to the top of the organization is no longer the primary goal. Equally important, the 24-hour news cycle, business television, high profile CEOs and the like have made companies more reactive to external perception. This has led to more change, fewer pension plans, and less job stability. No longer is it enough to get hired at company X, work there for 35 years and get a nice pension on which to retire.

The financial realities have made companies cut costs, cutting benefits alongside, and lifetime employment is gone. With no lifetime employment, employees have become about "What's in it for me?", though companies still want them to use John F. Kennedy's famous quote, morphed to business, as a guiding principle: "Ask not what we can do for you but what you can do for us."

Talent, which has always been scarce, has become mobile. The baby boomers haven't accepted this, and the Gen Ys haven't been able to articulate why.

When you don't expect to keep a job for life, greener grass means action. Money matters of course; most people won't change jobs for a lateral move at the same pay. Typically, a 10-15% raise is a given. But more often than not, it's not why you start looking. You are miserable. You don't like your boss. And when you are mobile, happiness and contentment become of greater importance.

"The company has decided to move you to Midland, Texas."

"The David has decided to quit."

Now, I am not advocating for a utopian society full of happy people who love what they do and laugh and run through the meadows with their co-workers and boss singing "It's a Wonderful World." I am, however, making the bold statement that happiness is a reasonable expectation--that sucking it up and taking one for the team and hoping for change is not a good choice.

Many people wake up every day dreading the drive to work, fantasizing about the weekend, and can't stand the people they work with. Be honest with where you are and what you can do.

I worked my ass off, fought for my people, helped created a billion (yes, billion) dollars of value, and got fired for my trouble. What I remember are the people I worked with, the projects I enjoyed, and the many, many hours I spent totally miserable, fighting for change that I could not bring about. If I learned anything, it's that if I want to run the company, set the course, and create the vision, I must do it from scratch.

Have the serenity to accept that companies cannot change, have the courage to change those things around you that impact your happiness, and the wisdom to know when to leave.

If I can impart some wisdom, and it is the only thing you remember from this book, then I will have been successful. I totally believe and feel very passionate that one must stop defining one's self by who one work for or what one does at work. Celebrate who you are and the choices you have made.

It isn't important what other people think of you (and in reality, they are only asking so that they can tell you about what they do). And for goodness sake, if you are a stay at home parent, stop apologizing for it.

After I got fired, the house roles began to shift. I am a horrible house husband. I don't clean, I don't cook, I rarely do laundry and when I do, I don't fold it. The benchmark by which I am measured is "Are the kids still alive?" When the answer to that question was yes, I had successfully fulfilled the role by the standards set for me. My point is--if you are a stay at home parent, it's friggin' hard. It's the hardest thing I have ever done and the thing at which I truly failed.

You are more valuable to the work world when you have stayed home and then choose to reenter the work force. You can deal with totally irrational and emotional human beings while at the same time have total power over them and elect to grow them rather than crush them. As with your kids, people rely on you and you never let them down. That kind of person is someone with whom I want to work.

Stop defining yourself by what you do. It's who you are that matters far more. And when you don't care what others think about what you do, you are free to find a place in the universe where you are happy doing what you do and being who you are.

[A refreshed and no doubt more succinct version of the same message.

***

Not that you need my permission, but you have it. You absolutely, positively should not care what others think of you if what you are doing is working.

Did you know that Rick Barry, a 10 season NBA Hall of Famer, shot 89.98% on free throws during his career? Underhand. In fact, he's the number 4 free throw shooter of all time, a feat he accomplished shooting granny style. Can you imagine the $hit he took every game? But- it made his team better and they won the 1975 NBA Championship while he won the MVP en route to getting into the Hall of Fame. So, you know what.... haters can go fornicate with themselves....

So the next time someone questions why you do something a certain way or you feel like you should want their approval, think of my man Rick *Barry.*

#hottakeoftheday, July 21 2019]

Lesson Two

A Tour of the Library

I remember the first week of my MBA for a lot of reasons, not just the investment banker who had rocked my world by suggesting that companies might, and, in fact, *should* fail.

I was about six years into my career, which is the optimal time to take an MBA, if you are asking for my opinion. My friend Jackie believes that it's eight. Maybe it's seven. Importantly, as I have the pen, I decree six years. It is known.

At this point, you have been out of your undergraduate program for long enough to appreciate school. I know that some people travel for a year in between high school and university and it helps them gain perspective and they value the university experience more, but I think that appreciation comes as much from maturity as experience.

In your career, you have seen enough at work to understand the interplay of all the pieces--management, finance, strategy, accounting, project teams, compensation plans, but you still have enough gaps in your knowledge to make learning the technical elements of these components relevant.

An MBA, and in my opinion, especially an executive MBA, is an excellent way to fill fissures in your knowledge and gives you credibility on the work front that will make you a more viable candidate for stretch roles. I believe that it shows initiative, but it is far more important you take an MBA because you want to learn--not because you want to get promoted. There are far easier ways to get promoted and if you don't use the knowledge and enjoy the process, I'm not sure it's worth it.

Chad, of Staten Island fame, probably put it best when I asked him what he thought of his MBA: "It's a tour of the library. You find out where all the books are, but you have to commit to continually going back." Very insightful, I thought anyway. Much better than his musings on fashion to be sure.

Getting an MBA is about life-long learning, so if you don't stretch yourself to continue to grow after the program, you are no better off than somebody with a library card who never goes to the library.

But there is another part to that, as the title of this chapter suggests. The school of experience has an entirely different curriculum; a curriculum that is found in the books that they hide from the students; the books you can only find in the basement behind the bodies. Sometimes they are funny; other times they are callous. But they matter just as much as the main curriculum. They teach you how to act in the line of fire. I have gone frequently into the basement; all the best books are there anyway.

I was down there just last week and was reminded of a book on email called *Unsubscribe Me, Please.* Email is a finicky thing because you don't have to be in the same room as the person to whom you are talking. For some, it enables you to write things you would never dare say in person to anyone.

It also means that you can participate in conversations with approximately thirty-eight people from different departments at any given time without having to call a meeting. How amazing! Often, people like to use the amazing 'Reply All' feature so everyone on the list can be educated as to what they are thinking. This, too, can go on for hours with hundreds of emails. Occasionally, if I was feeling cheeky, I would hit 'Reply All' and enter "Unsubscribe" into the subject line. It usually worked.

Alternately, email can also prove a challenge because the things that people have said or have asked for are very often included in the email you get when the request has been bounced around. Very often the text can include things such as: "So-and-so is useless and can't do their job. Can you get me the information? Thanks."

So-and-so is often the only person who can get the information and then usually discovers that they are useless, which leads them to not do their job and not get you the information.

Finally, email can magnify faults/challenges because you:

a) Say things you would never say in person
b) Have a "Forward" command
c) Have a "Reply All" command
d) Don't use them correctly

This is important because when you do use "Reply All" instead of "Forward" and include your personal thoughts like "Can you believe this guy, what a F@&KING idiot?", it also goes back to said idiot.

[Until I re-read the book for one last edit (the time after the last edit before that), I had forgotten about the beginnings of my views on email etiquette. By far, the most viewed post to date for the #hottakeoftheday was this one. As it turned out, it got 530,000 views in 5 days with almost 600 comments and 3,600 likes. I guess that's what it means to go viral.

The backstory was that I had just seen an email sent by a senior person in an organization with a lot of ccs, most of them junior staff. It was sent at 10:30 pm, I guess to show how hard the sender was working. At the time, I was texting my mother who was going through chemo (all good now) and I saw it. I was frustrated by the email because a) there was no need to send it at that time other than to show they were still working and b) nothing could be done about it, and it wasn't an emergency (emergencies are phone calls and everyone has their phone by their bed). My view now, having sent enough 10:30 pm emails in my life to realize what an asshole thing it was to do, is to use the "delay send" feature and have it hit their inbox in the morning. With that in mind, I penned this:

***

Some advice: Stop sending emails at 10:30 at night. Your poor time management all day should not cause me stress before I go to bed. There is software that allows the email to send the next morning. I'm really glad it's off your mind... but don't be selfish.

If you really want to impress people with how hard you work, send it at 2 pm so I can do something about it while I'm sitting at my desk.

#hottakeoftheday, May 18, 2019]

A couple years ago, I found a book called *Retired, A Euphemism for Being Fired.* My dad "retired" when I was thirteen, so he was around a lot. He had been a successful oil and gas executive who retired at 49, which to all my friends meant we were incredibly rich, and my father didn't have to work again.

When your friends tell you that you are rich and you are quite certain that your parents have shittier cars than everyone else, there is a disconnect. When there is a disconnect and you are wired like I am, you tend to ask questions to resolve the disconnect. I remember to this day the exact wording my dad used: "David, I've made enough money that every dollar I make from this point forward will go to your sister and you, and I'm not comfortable with that."

In the days that followed my firing, I remember how I felt about work and working for other people. If my two sons had been old enough to understand it, I'm pretty sure I would have used the exact same words.

After I got fired and I stopped watching the movie *Horrible Bosses* for inspiration, I stumbled across a book called *Getting Fired Is Rebirth.* It was written by a kooky philosopher who had originally written it for the core course curriculum, but some administrator (who was probably in charge of tuition) had thought it was too depressing to tell the MBAs who were paying $100,000 to be there. "I, an MBA graduate, can actually get fired?!?" I suppose that's how the author ended up in the basement; if you listen closely you can hear him wailing and dragging chains.

When you get fired, the question (after you get through the little matters of income, health care, telling your partner/kids/friends) you ask is "What the F@&K am I going to do? Am I in the right industry? The right city? The right role?"

It is the one time you don't get to weigh the options: Should I leave this job to go to XYZ company? How much am I leaving on the table? Is my salary better? How will my work/life balance be? What about my friends/colleagues?

Career-wise, I am convinced that rebirth can only happen when you've been fired. Now, you could go back to being exactly the same way you had been before. But for me, had I resigned when I had offered to three months before being fired, I wouldn't have been crushed. I wouldn't have taken the first job I could find. I wouldn't have had 16 months of transition to go through the stages of finding myself. And I wouldn't be here right now. So it certainly was a rebirth for this David and I hope it was for our other David. Speaking of, I did notice that Home Depot has a very well-worded warning on the container of its residential paint stripping chemicals. Step 1: Make sure it's your house.

I do get out of the library occasionally. I was recently at a funeral which happened to be on the campus where I pursued my MBA. After the service and a wonderful eulogy, my mind wandered back to my MBA and to the attendees who were milling about the conference center. What would I say to them if I were delivering a lecture? What could I teach them?

I have been fortunate to work at huge companies, medium-size companies, small companies as well as interact with service companies, consultancies, startups, and everything in between. The oil and gas industry is unique in that way because there is a niche and an opportunity for everyone. Competition is like that in professional sports: You compete to win--at auctions, at acquisitions, at public market perception--but you leverage your peers' knowledge, infrastructure, and, at times, training programs, to get the best results.

It is an unusual industry in that we don't set the price. Not even close. The market is so fractured that the largest players have no control over the price of the commodity, unlike software companies, consumer goods, and the like.

At times, it has been frustrating to watch companies that have made horrible decisions, run their people into the ground, but have simultaneously been incredibly successful because the commodity price was in a boom cycle. Conversely, it is difficult to stomach that no matter how many incredible decisions you make, when the commodity goes against you, you get absolutely crushed.

It is an industry that isn't well understood, but that I personally think is one of the greatest in which to work. It lives at the interface of science, of technology, of innovation and supplies the world with a commodity it couldn't live without. I am fortunate to work in this industry; I love it; I learn every day, and financially, I do ok. It is wonderful to be able to say I love what I do.

In final book of this adventure, I hope I can share my experiences over the past fifteen years; experiences of success, frustration and interacting with everyone else to giving you a tour of the basement of the library, where tough decisions, politics, lack of inspiration and real world leadership principles join forces with strategy, finance and management theories.

Lesson Three

Executive Summary

Unlike engineering school, business school at least understands that "It depends." is the answer to every question. A cynic would say that "It depends." means they don't know the answer. A philosopher would say they want you to discover the answer. It depends.

I have often thought about the last eighteen months of my life and tried to boil it down into a lecture or an elevator speech so I can share the $2.4 million of learning I've had in bite size pieces. One of the things that didn't "depend" in business school was the use of PowerPoint to share your story. Good slides have a title, four bullets at most and less than a line per bullet. I have used PowerPoints to document my work for years--it's a great way to organize your thoughts and, when it comes down to it, makes it really easy to present with no preparation.

Like the first chapter, bullets don't sell well. But for those of you who have made it this far, you can feel rewarded. You have found the purpose of the book. I even titled it "Executive Summary" to make it easy for you to refer to.

My PowerPoint looks like this:

Slide 1: It's easy to see how you got to where you are, but you really have no idea where you are going to end up. Life makes more sense in the rear-view mirror.

Slide 2: Don't reinvent the wheel. Take people's advice and integrate it into your thinking. If they are smart, you should know they are smart, and you should take their advice, even if you don't like what they have to say.

Slide 3: Just because you are good at "X", does not mean you can start a successful company. Starting a company takes the right people at the right time during the right economic circumstances, and, most importantly, luck.

Slide 4: Don't do it for the money. Do it because you love it. The money will follow good people and, eventually, you will make what you deserve.

Slide 5: When you can feel red flags, there are red flags. Do something about it. (more in Lesson Eight)

Slide 6: If you have to pick up the phone more than once to raise money, you shouldn't be raising money. (more in Lessons Nine and Ten)

Slide 7: Do not--under any circumstances--believe that you are more or less than you are based on the results of what you are doing. You are who you are, and you are judged by how you treat people, not by how much money you make (or lose). Results and money are two different things.

Slide 8: Work with people you respect. If you go down the entrepreneurial path, start a company with people you know

EXTREMELY well. Can you imagine marrying someone after one interview? Exactly.

Slide 9: Revenue equals good (don't reject new business because it doesn't fit the initial plan). Expenses equals bad (don't hire more people than you need until you absolutely need them).

Slide 10: Roll with the punches. There are a lot of ups and downs in life and no book can prepare you for it. It's all about attitude.

Slide 11: It could be the next meeting that changes your life.

Lesson Four

The Best Management Tip I Know

One of the bosses I had when I was much younger and at a huge company had a phenomenal way of bringing you into his group.

He was an intense guy--way more so than me, certainly. Which is hard to believe, but again, I can't make this stuff up.

Bald; huge goatee; loved guns. He made eye contact as though breaking it would have meant something bad. Even for me, who was not intimidated easily, Shane was a piece of work.

It turns out that he was one of the best bosses I ever had. One of the things he did for everyone who started working for him was hand out a one-page summary of his philosophy, beliefs, and how to understand him better. I always thought it was one of the best management tools I'd ever come across. Here's mine, I hope it helps.

Leadership Philosophy: Create a positive and energetic work environment; surround myself with people smarter than myself and harness their talent; and leave a lasting legacy for those who follow.

Leaders Do:

1. Serve to clear roadblocks and attract the resources necessary to be successful.
2. Guide and direct to stay within the confines of the overall strategy- the "what."
3. Communicate openly at all times and provide the "why" of decisions.
4. Focus on the process to ensure the results follow.

Leaders Don't:

1. Act as a roadblock or constrain the freedom of creativity of those they lead.
2. Offer the "how" before hearing and incorporating people's feedback.
3. Hide information or believe that their interests are more important than anyone else's.
4. Focus on results without understanding the sustainability of the process.

Hot Buttons:

1. Saying "no" to a solution without providing an alternative one.
2. Dishonesty or lack of transparency.
3. Not believing we ALWAYS have a choice in how we behave or what we do.

Strengths:

1. Seeing the "big picture" and prioritizing work to meet the overall strategy.
2. Energy level and work ethic.
3. Outside-the-box problem solving.

Weaknesses (I'm working on them!):

1. Patience.
2. Talking about D or E, before I have thoroughly explained A, B and C. (i.e. Going too fast when I get excited and see the end point.)
3. Office politics—I'm not as sensitive as I need to be.

Favorite Quotes:

"Facts are stubborn things and whatever may be our wishes, our inclinations, or the dictates of our passions, they cannot alter the state of facts, and evidence." - John Adams, 2nd President of the U.S.

"A man must be big enough to admit his mistakes, smart enough to profit from them, and strong enough to correct them." - John Maxwell

"Plans are only good intentions unless they immediately degenerate into hard work." - Peter Drucker

---

If you have people that work for you, and want to know what you stand for, I think it's worth doing. Hope it helps.

Lesson Five

Perception and Polar Bears

People have said "Perception is Reality". I think it depends from whose view that statement is being made. You making it about someone else: Reality. Someone else, making it about you: Perception.

A friend of mind--let's call him John--once said that when he and his wife were making love, he always felt as though he was riding in on the cavalry, sword drawn, and looking quite dramatic. Perception.

It wasn't until he and his love saw themselves on film (a decision made late one night after a few bottles of wine) that he recognized that instead of the cavalry, he looked like a cold polar bear, shivering in the night. Reality.

Perhaps a better example is the city I now call home: Denver. Whenever I'm travelling, there seems to be a perception that Denver is cold, snowy and otherwise the poor man's California. I had been here for four months, travelling back and forth between Calgary, and as the temperature started to drop in Calgary, it remained extremely pleasant in Denver. As people began to bring out their winter jackets, I was continuing to wear T-shirts. To someone who has been in a colder climate for most of his young life, Denver is a veritable tropical island.

My perception, which was different from the rest of the world it would seem, was that the clips I had seen on the national news that were usually of massive amounts of snow in Denver were very, very rare.

For 300 days a year, Denver is sunny. For most of those days, if there is snow, it is gone within a day or two, but is seldom more than a one-half inch. *Most* of those days.

I remember when I moved here in 2006. It was December 21st, my family was still in Canada, and I was about to catch my last flight home before 2007.

I went to the office as usual. But not as usual, there was mass panic. A snowstorm was coming to Denver that very day. I looked outside. It was 34 F, the sky was grey, but there was nothing ominous. It was the same as it had been for two or three days--perhaps warmer--and I thought "These wussies! I'm from Canada. We have snow. We have cold. You get scared over a little winter storm?!"

So, I put my head down and worked. By 10 a.m., the email went out that the office would be closing in thirty minutes…. Are you F@&KING serious?!? I started laughing but the exodus was complete by 10:37 a.m. The office was empty. Except for me, who was living in a hotel four blocks away and had nowhere to go. Plus, I'm Canadian. I know snow.

Having uninterrupted time to work is one of life's great pleasures when your day is full of meetings, requests, and people idly chatting. I worked solidly for four hours without looking up. I was having the time of my life, productive, reinventing the wheel at least four times. I was happy. Finally, with my back aching, I stood up to walk around and look out the window. Sure enough. Snow. Big heavy flakes in the air. Impressive. Snowy. But office closure? Are you kidding me? So back to work I went.

By 4:30 p.m. that afternoon, I felt that I had accomplished a lot and I was excited to get to the hotel, have a workout and a nice steak. I grabbed my bag and headed for the door. In my suit. Dress shoes. Ready for summer.

The shock that met me when I hit the main floor is unlike anything I had ever experienced. Approximately two feet of snow had come down. In five hours. What the F&@K?! I mean, Day after Tomorrow kind of stuff. There was not a car, not a person, nothing in sight. The entire downtown was deserted. Not a single tire track on the road, no footprints on the sidewalk. Restaurants closed. Abandoned.

The airport was closed for three days. I almost didn't make it back to Canada for Christmas with my family.

My perception was that people from Denver didn't understand snow. In fact, it was me who didn't have the experience to understand that kind of snow fall.

This is important when it comes to organizations. Impolitely, they can be like monkeys in a tree. Everyone looking down sees nothing but smiles and everyone looking up sees nothing but assholes. That's personal perception. Know where you are and know what people think of you. Then go about taking action to make changes.

Then there is the perception of roles, responsibilities, division of labor and the like. Have you ever talked to your boss about your role or workload? More often than not, if you haven't said anything, they assume you are underworked, and new accounts come to you. The perception is you are happy. The reality is you don't have time to talk to anyone because you keep getting new accounts.

Don't assume that anyone in the organization understands what you do, or how long it takes you to do it. Set weekly meetings with your boss just to have a check-in. Pre-schedule the meeting so that it's on the calendar and there doesn't need to be a topic, just a check-in.

Have at least a quarterly meeting with your bosses' boss, alone if you can, to make sure that two layers up in the organization has the same understanding of what you are working on.

Organizations can be like a game of telephone. Remember the one that went around the circle and you were supposed to repeat word-for-word what you heard and by the end of the game the message is entirely morphed? Put politics into play, with selfishness and bad leadership, and this problem gets much larger.

Let's talk about face time. Now, I must admit I have been out of a company for eighteen months so I either have perspective or lethargy. But the thought of staying at the office to "impress" your boss is absolutely ridiculous. If your boss needs to "see you" then your boss has problems. You either do your job or you don't. If you don't, then you should know in your heart you aren't putting in all your effort and that you aren't performing. Being at the office "just because" is unnecessary.

If you are a person who understands the big picture and the nature of the job, being told to count the crumbs you generate after you eat a piece of toast is as ridiculous as it sounds. I don't have a strategy to tell your boss that it's a waste of time, and I don't have a recommendation that looks like just ignoring the request, but when organizations wear the tires off people "just because", it's not a company of which you want to be a part. There is a difference between good technical evaluation and overkill, and there is a time for both. But if your boss and your company don't know the difference between important, unimportant, urgent and interesting, it's time to start looking for a new company.

[As I read this today, I realize that this view is a little utopian and reflects the state of the oil and gas industry in 2013 when it was the ultimate boom time. In 2019 unfortunately, the balance of power has shifted and while being principled is essential, having a job can be more important. So, while I still wholeheartedly agree with this assessment of face time, I concede that if your boss doesn't agree with this view and you need income, this is one of those times where you have to accept that being correct and being employed might be at odds].

Lesson Six

Every Deal Is Different

"Deals" are the dream of every MBA student. You learn finance, strategy, accounting, and all other manner of skillsets in which to "do deals" and then you are sent into the world armed with the tools but still have no idea how to really use them. Nothing battle-tests, wounds, and attempts to mortally injure you like an active deal does because it goes nothing like the way it was conjured up in your head.

In your mind, a deal is identified, and you have access to all the data and financials that allow you to work through the company or assets in a methodical and measured way. You have a team of specialists, hopefully ten or more who are all working together in a collaborative manner, sharing finds and evaluating discoveries over a two-month period. At the end of the two months, you submit a strong, fairly valued bid. The company calls you and says "Congratulations, you are the successful bidder." You sign a letter of intent and you issue a press release that announces you have successfully come to a win – win solution and everyone is jubilant over the results.

In reality, it is an absolute cluster-F@&K that follows none of those steps. Instead, it is a bumbling and terrifying process that feels like a roller coaster ride that eventually leaves you in a puddle of goo, lying on your computer keyboard hoping for a sword and a clean death. It is also important to note they take significantly longer than you even think possible and I would estimate only one in ten actually get across the finish line.

In my career, I have been fortunate to have been a part of a number of deals. I witnessed some from the stands, some on the sidelines as the occasional substitution, and more recently a number from the cockpit. I have been continually and consistently surprised at how they progress.

Many of the stories I will share have been recounted from many sources over the past seven years and so take everything I recount with a grain of salt, or an entire shaker. I share the stories because they are interesting, at least to me, and on the heels of many of the deals I had seen earlier in my career, I think it spells out the thesis of the chapter--every deal is different, and you can't fathom how they will ever actually get done.

The biggest, best known, and probably most interesting of the deals I have been privy to be a part of was the Anadarko acquisition of Kerr-McGee and Western Gas, simultaneously. Two companies with two offers that totaled $23 billion dollars in cash by a company that at the time had a market cap of $22 billion and an enterprise value (equity plus debt) of approximately $26 billion.

I was two weeks from starting my MBA that was to be paid for by the same company. It was a mere $100,000, so it was somewhat lost in the decimal places of the transaction. Twice before in my career, companies I had been with were part of some sort of acquisition process: In 1998, the summer after my painting adventures, oil prices cratered and the company I was working at as a marketing summer student was effectively bankrupt. I showed up for work only to discover that there had been a press release issued that morning announcing that we were being purchased. I had no idea what that meant in practical terms, but all of the expense accounts were frozen and the whole office came to a complete standstill. I just remember going to the bar at about 10 a.m. with half of the office and sitting outside on the patio drinking all day and then going out all night. At the time, it seemed like a fantastic way to spend the day!

The second time was the company with whom I did my internship. They had completed an Initial Public Offering about a year before I started (in 1999 when gas prices were rebounding off the lows and the commodity boom for natural gas was in full force.) The company went public at around $8 and sold in 2001 for $53 a share to Burlington Resources, a huge U.S. independent oil and gas producer. What I didn't discover until ten years later was that there had been suitors for the company constantly from 1999 – 2001. In 2000, it rebuffed an offer for about $25 a share to Burlington, and it was a very difficult decision for senior management to make. The only thing that saved them was they knew this offer was out there and they issued a press release discussing the portfolio and all the value they stood to unlock over the following few years. The market absolutely loved it and drove the stock up, something that would continue to happen for the next year. Finally, the acquisition was announced when the stock was at $36 a share and garnered a huge premium

What I remember particularly vividly was the impact on stock options. Options are compensatory incentives that provide employees leverage to an improving stock price. They usually "vest" over a number of years, except in the case of a change in control, as is the case of an acquisition. The one person I remember specifically was a senior drilling engineer who had left Anadarko to join Canadian Hunter the previous week, worked for a mere three days, then had his options vest for almost one million dollars. Not bad for a week's work.

It was the era for mergers in the oil and gas industry, and I didn't have to wait long for my new company to get into the mix. I'd been at Anadarko for about five weeks. At the time, a very famous Canadian oil tycoon had a company by the name of Berkley Petroleum, and they had assets across Western Canada and California. A private U.S. company made a hostile takeover offer and Berkley responded by rejecting the offer and opening up a data room looking for a "White Knight." A hostile takeover doesn't come with any of the niceties of working collaboratively with the management team, as the Burlington acquisition of Canadian Hunter did. During a hostile takeover attempt, you are shut out of the data and, more often than not, it gets acrimonious as senior management at the target company does everything in its power to stop you from taking over.

Searching for a White Knight involves opening a data room and letting anyone and their dog, except the hostile party, in to see all your documents and come up with a more compelling value for the company. Anadarko was that White Knight and we ended up with Berkley and their entire staff.

Most of the technical teams remained totally intact from the pre-merger company. They knew the assets better than any of the staff from the acquiring company, so they were left alone to run the assets while their founder got an advisory management position and was at the table to approve all the funding decisions.

Having just started, I was put on one of the acquired asset teams with one other new graduate, so I had a front row seat. Immediately, the culture clash was apparent. I laugh now looking back at how surprised I was, but it was palpable.

In the simplest terms, there are big company people and there are little company people. Little company people are used to moving fast, thinking fast, executing fast and dreaming of selling to a big company so that they can do it again. It is an over-simplification of course, but useful to consider in this particular case. If you take these same people and have them work for a slow-moving company with an entire team dedicated to budget exercises, who has forecasts and reforecasts every month, and weekly meetings to approve any and all capital decisions you want to make, and there is a clash.

More to the point, Berkley was fending off a hostile takeover and so every asset they had had some incredible value creation opportunity, if only we would execute on it. As the buyer, we bought the story that every asset had an incredible value opportunity if only we would execute on it.

Processes weren't in place; assets were over-promised and under-delivered, and the lipstick soon wore off the pig. Having been at Canadian Hunter, probably the premier independent energy company in Canada, I, too, assumed that all their assets were wonderful and valuable and acquiring companies knew what they were buying. They were not and they do not. That is why the history of mergers and acquisitions in all industries is littered with disasters: AOL-Time-Warner probably tops the list but there are countless others.

Eventually, Anadarko spun out a small, unloved asset that they had acquired to the founder of Berkley. Duvernay was started and over time took most of the team that had worked at Berkley prior to the merger, went public and Anadarko made a small gain and then sold to Shell in 2008 for $5 billion--five times the value of what Anadarko had bought Berkley at in 2001.

I didn't learn then, but I now know three things.

One, when you have a great team, it is very hard to replicate so teams that are successful should stay together, one way or the other.

Two, those that know how the system works and how to make money, do it repeatedly and successfully over the course of time.

Three, when you have a track record like the founder of Berkley did, he can raise money like no other and when you can raise money, eventually good things will happen. Opportunity is what happens when the well-prepared get lucky.

By 2006, Anadarko had discovered that the businesses it had bought in Canada through the Union-Pacific merger in 1999 and Berkley in 2001 did not have the portfolio it needed to be meaningful. The U.S. portfolio was also faltering and was noted by its big Gulf of Mexico development Marco Polo. Marco Polo was significantly less prolific than was expected and the company had fallen from Wall Street's graces.

Jim Hackett, a man whom I idolized, was the CEO of Anadarko and is perhaps the most well-spoken, charismatic CEO I have ever seen. He is definitely a "Rock Star CEO" and so when I first met Jim in 2003, I was awestruck. Jim had merged Seagull with Ocean Energy and then orchestrated the merger of Devon and Ocean prior to leaving and joining Anadarko.

Al Walker, the now-CEO, had a successful career in the financial industry and was at Seagull prior to joining 3Tec, which subsequently got acquired by Plains Exploration in 2003. At that time, Al joined an investment bank in Houston and was there until rejoining Jim, now at Anadarko in 2005.

As the story goes, there was a come-to-Jesus management meeting in 2005 where results weren't what was expected of the company and the Executive Committee lost it. I wasn't at the meeting, but it was recounted often, with many different impressions and reactions. The unattributed quote that was consistently used to highlight the contents of that meeting was: "Give me one F@&KING reason we shouldn't sell this company and fire everyone here?!" Phew! I admit I dodged a bullet not being in that particular meeting, the story second and third hand was scary enough.

As legend has it, Al and Jim were neighbors (relatively speaking), and Al, who was working at that investment bank, pitched Jim on a deal. That deal was Kerr-McGee. Jim responded to Al that he didn't have anyone who could run it. Al suggested "I can do it" and joined Anadarko as CFO. The next year, Kerr-McGee and Anadarko were merged.

Concurrently, Anadarko's business development group was working with the technical team to buy Western Gas, a small player in the Rockies that had excellent midstream assets and a premier position in two of Wyoming's major gas plays.

Two great deals, why not? Let's just buy them both. The deals were funded through a consortium that included the investment banks, who according to the same legend made approximately $60 million in fees so as hiring goes, it was probably one of the better returns on investment in the history of investment banking hires.

The Canadian division of Anadarko, where I was at the time, was sold to pay down debt and announced in September, three months later. By the end of that month, I had been moved to Denver to help integrate three companies with 1,000 employees in a city in which Anadarko had no office.

Over the next six months, asset plans were put together, divestiture candidates were identified, and the infamous reorganization was looming. My boss--the one who had supported my MBA, the one who had had me moved to Denver, the one whom I credit with much of my early success and who saved me from becoming an investment banker in 2006--was fantastic throughout the process and miraculously kept everyone calm and focused on execution. And then, one day in January, he announced that he and all but one of the leadership team he had formed in September, only five months previous, would be leaving the company. From my seat, most of the senior roles were given to former Kerr-McGee leaders and the merger was complete.

I had always assumed that it was Anadarko who had bought Kerr-McGee, when in fact it was the other way around. Kerr-McGee had a portfolio of some of the best assets in North

America's onshore gas plays, and its Gulf of Mexico position was complementary to Anadarko.

Flash forward to 2013, Anadarko spun out the Western Gas midstream assets into a master limited partnership (MLP); the Wattenberg position that came from Kerr-McGee houses one of the best horizontal oil plays in the U.S. (though no one knew about it in 2006); Anadarko's international exploration finally hit and has led to some world class discoveries; the Eagle Ford and Marcellus were discovered post- transaction where Anadarko had put together a huge land position. It has been an unreal success story, but not for the reasons that anyone thought in 2006 when an onshore gas portfolio was the most coveted portfolio in North America. Anadarko even sold its Bakken position to keep more exposure to gas and the Bakken is the hottest play in the industry today.

So, there you have it, I was six years into my career and had just witnessed more than $30 billion in transactions. I thought I'd seen it all, but I was just getting started.

[As the book continues, you will see I hadn't seen it all. Not even close. It's why when people reach out to me and say "I want to be in Business Development" I say, it's not something you do, it's something you learn, and you are always learning.

***

It's official: I have a new crush and it's Vicki Hollub. She is one tough, creative and feisty cookie and I like it a lot!

In the span of 2 weeks, Oxy has gone from unrequited admirer trying to get Anadarko's attention to superhero calling all the shots. I thought the Buffet play was creative – a touch expensive but hey, the things we do for love.

But now…. pre selling an asset they don't even own in the largest risk area of the deal's integration to raise cash and leave the 3- D's behind (DJ, Delaware, Deep Gulf of Mexico)…. be still my beating heart!

I love when companies stop playing by some antiquated and outdated rules designed to keep incumbent management teams in control of a process when they should be maximizing shareholder value instead. Elliot Management started strong in QEP but faded fast and appears to have lost without even a fight (the last press release on that deal was January!!) but this…. this is incredible.

So, here's to you Madame Hollub. Can't wait to see what you do next.

#hottakeoftheday, May 6th, 2019]

Lesson Seven

Moving into the Cockpit

I left Anadarko in 2009, three years after the merger. I didn't deal particularly well with being on the losing side of the transaction and by losing, I mean it figuratively. My champions, my friends, and those who had been so supportive of me were out. Although I had been in Canada and away from Anadarko "U.S." for the first five years, it pained me to feel so slighted. We bought them, didn't we? Kerr-McGee employees cashed their options in and got new options, right? They should be leaving the company and we should run things the Anadarko way, whatever that was. What the F@&K is wrong with everybody else? I think that may have been when I first started asking that.

I didn't fit in. At the time, I thought it was because I was a former Anadarko guy, which may have been partly the case. The reality, however, was that I wasn't a big company guy--I just didn't know it yet. It sounds silly, I know. All my friends knew it and everyone I worked with knew it, I just had a huge blind spot.

I managed to stay for two and a half years before I got a call from a headhunter. I picked up the phone. "How'd you like to help a

Canadian company fix its U.S. subsidiary and lead the operations and business development effort for them?" It wasn't on a clipboard but how could I refuse? That was how I joined BakkenCo.

During my three years there, I was fortunate to play a major part in three major transactions and have a front row seat in a fourth. Each of these deals were totally different, but they all emerged in a related way. And not one went down the way we thought they would.

It was 2009 and the Bakken craze in North Dakota was just ramping up. It was still a very new play and industry didn't understand it particularly well, thus making it hard to imagine what it would eventually become. As we sit in 2013, it is the premier oilfield in North America with ~$25 billion a year being spent in that state to drill, complete, and produce oil wells in the Bakken formation. It's staggering that a play could and can go from unknown to this in four years.

At BakkenCo, we targeted the Bakken and the Marcellus as the two emerging plays and set out to acquire a position. In the Bakken, the asset for which I was responsible, the only part of the play available at that time was in between two very active and prolific fields. If you drew a line between the two and compared the geology, you would find them to be pretty similar, so there was absolutely no reason there should be a "hole" right in the center of the play. Unless, of course, it was on an Indian Reservation. Which it was. And since there were very few companies in the entire history of oil and gas that had good experiences there, the only companies that were willing to pursue "the hole" were private companies and private equity-backed companies. The former not needing to worry about public perception and the latter being willing to go pretty much anywhere to get returns in excess of 25%.

And so, my private company began the slow and painstaking process of buying assets that weren't officially for sale. We were fortunate, however, since one of our board members for the Canadian publicly listed company was also a founder of a private equity company that actually helped internalize BakkenCo's management in the early 2000s. He suggested we talk to his firm about this small portfolio company they had that was looking to de-risk their position. We followed his advice.

It was an odd experience for me, having never dealt with anyone at a private company to that point. There were three guys. That was it. They had no wells, no revenue, and no production; only a few permits to drill and a few contractors. I called it "Three Guys and a Cell Phone." I think they might have had three cell phones, but it ruined the catch phrase. They later told me they also had a truck that they left in North Dakota. So now it was "Three Guys with Cell Phones and a Truck." And I forgot to mention one of the most desirable land positions in North Dakota.

It absolutely boggled my mind. How could this be? Where did their money come from? How did they know to buy it? How did they buy it? Where were all the people?

Their model was quite simple: Acquire the land, spend as little money as possible to show how much value there could be, and sell it to the highest bidder over the course of three years. We'll come back to this in a later chapter.

In my infinite big-company wisdom, I had heard that private equity firms are looking for a double (I laugh at this now.) So, our first offer to them was quite literally to take what they originally paid and multiply it by two. We would then own half the land and we could move forward as partners. We would "operate" (control the drilling, run the people, and perform all the work) while they would pay for their share and be happy to let us do it. They did, after all, have only three cell phones and a truck.

Laughter ensued when we brought forth our offer. When you are a small company guy, and a private equity backed company to boot, a double is actually not the target. The most money possible for the least risk is the target. After three months of negotiation, we settled on an amount that was ten times what they had paid for the land, give or take, and that would give them enough money to drill four wells. BakkenCo would design and help operate, but the "Three Guys and Cell Phones and a Truck" would be the actual operators. Being the operator ensures that you can sell the asset for the highest price at the end of the day. Operatorship is the number one requirement of PE-backed companies-you must control it.

Together with our partners, we drilled four wells over the next six months and the results were fantastic. BakkenCo ended up buying the second half of the deal as soon as the fourth well was finished, and this time paid twenty times what they originally paid. They had turned approximately $7.5 million into $125 million in just over two years. They made about $30 million between the three guys to pay for their cell phones and a couple of other nice toys. Freed from company A, they started company B about one month later, and two months after that, BakkenCo got a call from these three guys to see if we were interested in buying some land in the "Niobrara." The same "Niobrara" that was about six months away from taking off and becoming the jewel of Anadarko's portfolio. How the F@&k did they know to go there?

All the while, our goal wasn't the first or even the second acquisition--that was just to get us up the learning curve and establish ourselves in North Dakota. The crown jewel was the third transaction, which I started to work on the day after we closed the first 50% deal.

I was the most active non-operated partner in the history of oil and gas: I was involved in negotiations with the Indian tribe, with the infrastructure, electrical and pipeline build-outs, road construction, and I was leading the charge on technical improvements to well design. I would meet guys and they would say "I don't recognize BakkenCo, do you have any land?" "Sure do!" I would reply. We had less than 10% of the land that others had yet there I was, whether I was needed to negotiate something, break a stalemate, or just make things happen.

So, it was no surprise that I would soon become a close associate and friend of the Chairman of another PE-backed company-twice the size, a little bit better capitalized with a staff of fifteen and a few wells drilled. But most importantly, the company had a track record. This was the third company the same team was working on; the previous two had already sold and they were coming to the end of their three years with this company.

Ryan and I got along fabulously; we would talk on the phone once a week, catch up on all things happening on the reservation, and I learned a ton about the way he thought, the success he had and the way to start, build, and run a PE-backed company.

When it came time for them to sell, BakkenCo was one of only eight companies invited to "preview" the assets, before it became available to everyone. Eight? That sounds like an auction to me, but beggars can't be choosers. We wanted that asset--needed it actually--to really become meaningful in the company portfolio.

We bid on it and ended up winning. We paid 40x more than the land had been bought for (when you back out the capital that had been spent on drilling) and set a new high watermark for deals in the Bakken. It's now worth somewhere around 150x the original cost basis of the land.

There's nothing like the oil business.

At the closing dinner with all the senior executives at BakkenCo, myself included and those at Ryan's company (all three of them), Ryan gave a toast that credited me for making the deal happen. It was extremely touching and extremely dangerous. In front of all the senior executives at the company, all of whom were more senior than me, all of whom were taking credit for their role in the deal, I was named as being the one that made it happen. Whether it was the beginning of the end, whether it went to my head and I started ignoring what my senior peers wanted me to do, or whether it was a high compliment from someone I deeply respect, I don't know.

***

At a dinner in the years that followed my departure from BakkenCo, I was working on an entirely different deal and having a dinner with the senior leadership of a company that our new company, StartUpCo, was trying to transact with. Their senior vice president, whom I had never met before, didn't know that I had been with BakkenCo until it came up at the dinner. He looked at me and said:

"Please explain to me how you ended up with that Bakken deal when we bid more than you did?"

Oh. Now I know why Ryan gave me credit for the deal. We weren't the high bidder, and they had chosen to close with us. I don't know how much that cost Ryan out of his own pocket, or the other factors that went into that decision, but it did teach me a valuable lesson: It's not always about the dollars and cents, it's about relationships. If you don't have one, you better be prepared to pay a lot more than you thought you needed to.

$30 billion of deals I watched from the outside; $600 million of deals I was in the cockpit for. One would think I would have learned a thing or two by the time we started StartUpCo. One would have thought.

Lesson Eight

Red Flags are Red Flags, Even if You Were Just Fired

In the days that followed my firing from BakkenCo, I raced to get my career back on track. Subconsciously, I knew it was coming, so in November, a headhunter connected me with someone I had actually worked for (indirectly) as an intern in 1999. How does an intern end up in a leadership position with a new company thirteen years later? It probably happens more frequently these days at technology companies, but my image of interns is mostly shaped by Owen Wilson and Vince Vaughn in *The Internship.* It's absolutely hilarious if you like *Office Space* humor.

When I was the intern, it was 1999, and I was an engineering intern who had been doing stock research for his dad for four years. When I got my first job and they gave me the tools of the industry, I could actually analyze these companies down to a level of precision I could only dream of as a 16-year-old (in between dreaming of Cindy Crawford and Rachel Hunter).

So, with said tools in hand, one day after work, I put together a $150 million dollar proposal to buy a company. Just like that. I stayed at work until 2 a.m. writing the report. I ordered pizza and coke and had it delivered to security. It was my first official all-nighter, by my own choice, and I could hardly wait to do it again.

I was so convinced that it was a fantastic deal, I left the report on my boss' desk. When she didn't say anything that morning, I followed up at about 10 a.m. and said "Well, what did you think?"

"Ahh, I'm not sure what you want me to do with this. This isn't exactly why we hired you."

"We should give it to your boss."

Silence. Awkward silence.

"Ahh, okay."

So, we went to see her boss. I gave him the report and a brief summary of the deal, which by now I was convinced would be one of the best deals ever. It was, after all, nine hours since being completed. I was twenty-two. I knew what I was doing. Seemed obvious at the time.

He said "I'm not sure what you want me to do with this. This isn't exactly why we hired you."

Hmmmm, familiar....

"We should give it to your boss."

"Ahh, okay".

And so, at twenty-two, as an intern without a formal role in the company, I pitched this deal to the senior leadership of the company and ended up moving into Business Development putting deals together.

"Uh, do you work here?" "No. I'm just an intern." That was also how I got to know Michael. I was still fun, I believed the world was my oyster, and I may have been a little bit extreme.

Thirteen years later, Michael was still in Calgary and had a number of successful roles following the sale of Canadian Hunter in 2001. He was working with an M&A lawyer and co-founder of our company looking to start a "cross border trust"- a publicly listed Canadian company with U.S. assets. In November when they first "interviewed' me, they described the business plan, which was quite simple: Get funded, buy a big U.S. operated asset, run it for two years, and then go public at a premium.

It seemed reasonable on the surface, but there was something that didn't fit. How could you go from nothing to something, and that something being a $500 million dollar asset overnight? I liked the idea, but I wasn't ready to leave the company I was at, no matter how much of an asshole it was making me, so I wrote a memo and proposed a new business plan that would be more successful and offered to be on the board. Yep. I did that.

The memo talked about a value proposition and buying assets to capture arbitrage and was literally something you might expect out of Bain & Co, not a candidate for a VP job. But it was brain candy for me. I loved what I did, I was good at it, and I liked to be helpful. Or at least liked to think I was being helpful. You might not be an oil and gas person, which is fine. Like every industry, we use big complicated acronyms but it's all the same. Buy low, sell high, and do it better than everyone else. Picture yourself waiting to hear if a candidate was going to accept your offer of employment and instead you get a memo improving the business model.

I didn't think much of it until Wednesday, February 1st, 2012 at 4:37 p.m. I had been fired about an hour before. I was headed to my car on my way to give a squash lesson to a kid with whom I had been working with for about a year. A lesson I was seriously considering cancelling, given that I had just had my world shattered. But shock is a wonderful coping mechanism for the body--you can carry on as though nothing really happened. So, I went to the lesson and called the headhunter who had reconnected me with Michael.

"Beau, I need a job. Like today. Is Michael still looking?"

"Yes."

"I'll take it."

If you are about to be fired, and you are reading this book, please, don't do what I did. It was not a fit, red flags were going off in my head, and most importantly, I was good at what I did – I didn't need to take the first job I found. Take a moment, realize the world is not ending, and do what I talked about in the first chapter of this book. Lose some weight (ha!) and think about what it is you want to do for the rest of your life. It's the only time you get this perspective.

In hindsight, though, I'm glad I took the job for what I eventually learned and where I am today. Taking the job was the wrong decision overall. I hope this book, your experience, and superior decision-making skills can get you to where I am now without going through a goat rope.

Nonetheless, I did get fired, I did take the first job I found, I un-cancelled my part of the family trip to Hawaii and I was back.

It was a cluster F@&K from the start. The best lessons always are.

StartUpCo was founded to raise $300 million dollars from large pension funds and institutions so that we could acquire oil and gas assets in the United States, manage them as a private company for two years, and then, with a track record, we would go public. Sort of like going to a car lot, picking out a car, driving it for a while and then giving it to your kid. The analogy isn't perfect, but if you aren't in the oil and gas industry, it's a tangible comparison.

The plan was to have $300 million of committed financing by June, an asset by September, running privately for two years while creating a track record and spinning out $30 million a year in dividends and going public at a $500 million dollar valuation two years from now. It was a good plan, or so I wanted to think. Red flags, giant banners, and war drums were all beating in my head. And by beating, I mean hammering. But I was committed, and dammit, I wasn't going to fail again—not so soon after being fired!

On the team with Michael was also Jim, an older business development engineer, Grant, a finance guy, and Gerald, our operations guy.

Jim and I had similar roles, but completely different styles and personalities. Grant and Michael had similar backgrounds, and completely different personalities. Gerald was an operations guy and we had no operations. Nor did we have line of sight to operations.

Now that we had a U.S. team, Michael, Jim and I headed off to the biggest conference in the industry to introduce our new company to the world. So, there we were, armed with a sheet of paper that basically said we were looking for deals. $500 million was the perfect size. We had no financial backer. No assets. No staff. And no corporate credit card yet.

I arrived at the conference after some weeks of reflection in Hawaii, brimming with false hope and canned confidence. Ten paces into the conference center, I bumped into people I knew, not well, but well enough.

They had "heard the news", "How was I doing?", "Oh, you've already started somewhere?", "Tell me about it." And so, I did. As the words came out, it sounded hollow, and moreover, sounded like a horrible plan. That alone should have awakened me from my slumber to find something else.

As it turned out, I didn't wake up and instead I walked around mindlessly for two days. The conference ended. We didn't have any assets or leads. The only bright spot was the person I met that is my confirmation that meeting with people is never a waste of time, but that's a story for a later chapter.

I got back to Denver and I raced to find office space. All companies I know have an office and I was going to be no different. We were going to make it. And, quite frankly, I needed a place to go. I couldn't be the one to pick the kids up and drop them off! I was a F@&King oil and gas executive, dammit. I needed my life back.

While we didn't have a lot, we had plans to raise $4.5 million dollars, money that in truth I had thought had already been raised before I joined in February. Over the course of the next six weeks, I discovered that that wasn't the case.

“Great!”, I thought. “I get an opportunity to help raise the money and raise it from my friends and family who will get a great return!” And so, I did. And like my painting business, I can sell, and I did sell. And when it is to family and friends who trust me and know me and, quite frankly, just want to help me move past getting fired, they wrote big checks.

I had raised $450,000 from my closest family and friends in about a week, all of whom said variations of “You are the most tenacious mother F@&Ker I know. If there is anyone on earth, I want to put my money with, it’s you.”

That’s confidence; it’s also true. But I can tell you that while tenacity is a huge plus, it is not a guarantee of success--especially when you have a $1 million payroll, and a $1 million dollar G&A budget for computers, offices, travel and the like.

But these were merely details. We had a plan, I had trust and faith and naivety and self-belief combined with a wounded ego and absolutely no idea what the real world was like for startups.

So, for $2,000 a month, I got an office. Actually, an executive suite with two offices and a front sitting area for conferences. I was ambitious. We were going to be hiring people within months; we could pack in four before we needed to move. That was in March.

I started creating employee handbooks, compensation philosophy, identifying all the available deals and working round the clock. We were going to launch this bad boy within weeks. I was so excited.

The excitement didn’t last long.

By June, I barely went to the office which I had coveted so few months before. There was nothing that couldn't be done with a laptop and a cell phone remotely. There was nobody to see, we had no deals, no staff, no money, and no prospects of money. In fact, we hadn't had an institutional money-raising meeting in the first five months.

We did, however, create a 200-slide PowerPoint that was to be the pitch book. We practiced the presentation we would give. But we never actually gave it. No. Actually, that's not true. We gave it once. To an investor who was a friend of Michael's who thought he might be able to put $30,000 into the business. We needed $300 million. But we did give that presentation once.

It was at this point, Grant left. Jim and I couldn't stand to be in the same room together. Gerald was bored out of his mind and Michael and I had the first fight for control.

We hadn't delivered on the plan--specifically, presenting the pitch book or having money. I suggested that the burn rate was too high and that everyone should cut their salaries, including the board of directors who each got $30,000 a year in fees. Now, in fairness, they had each put in $100,000--or rather had committed to--but by June, they hadn't yet, and this was a huge bone of contention for me.

When you, a 35-year-old who had recently been fired, tells the founder with forty years of industry experience that the plan isn't working, salaries should be cut, and the board should resign unless they write the check they had committed to write, it doesn't go over well.

You get asked things like "Are you on board with this plan?" "It seems like you might not fit in." "Maybe it's time we part ways."

Now, in most circumstances, and especially if it had only been my $100,000, I would have been gone. As of last June, I would have found another job, after a four-month stint at a startup. I expect that I would have been disenfranchised with the whole thought of a startup and would have gone back to a large company. And I probably would have slogged my way through another three years before being fired again.

But fortunately for me now, and totally unfortunately then, there was the matter of my closest friends' $400,000. As it stood with only $1.6 million raised to that point in cash, this contribution made me approximately 30% owner of the firm. This was a far cry from the $4.5 million targeted, and it was looking more and more likely that not only were we not going to get to $4.5 million, but $1.6 million might be the actual number and we would be out of money by November.

My response was measured, for a change, and sounded something like "You are more than welcome to write me and my family and friends a check to reimburse our money and I will leave happily and quietly. But as things stand right now, I control 30% of the company, and there is no F@&KING way I'm leaving while that money stays."

That's when I started to golf. Every single day. There was nothing to do. I couldn't leave; I couldn't work aimlessly; I needed something to do and excel at and work my butt off at, so golf was it. Thus, I put all of my effort into golf. I managed to get my handicap legitimately from a 2 to a +2 (legitimate in golf means you actually write down your score). The summer was mostly spent on the golf course. Not officially, of course; that wouldn't play well. We had four in the office in Calgary, who could keep track of each other, but I was 1,000 miles away, a 30%

owner, working and thinking about it every second, and finding a more productive way of using my time than ranting at my co-workers about all the things we needed to do. I opted for patience. When the time came, I would be ready. But for now, I would relax and take some time to find myself.

I used my headphones and took calls from the golf course. When I hit the ball, I muted the line. I once shot a 70 and was on the phone for the entire round listening to a four-hour data room for an asset I already understood. I would chime in every twenty minutes or so and ask a few questions, then just listen and go back to my game.

Now, you might be thinking, well of course the business was failing. You weren't working.

On the contrary, I was working every hour. Work is a hobby. Deals are my favorite things to think about. When I am on the phone in the office, I pace all over. But the honest truth was I finally got to a place where we had no money, therefore we couldn't buy anything. If we couldn't buy anything, nothing that I screened and ranked and said, "This is the greatest thing in the world!" mattered because we had no money.

In July and August, we started sending our pitch book to investors, and our Chairman and CEO--both of whom were the original founders--actually met with people. We didn't get a lot of responses, but what the responses we did get some were all the same: "Great book. Where's your asset?"

"Well, you see, our plan was to get funding first, and then go find an asset."

"Bad plan. Go find an asset."

Oh. That sucks. I wish I would have known that in February or March or June or July or even August.

By September, we realized there was no way we could mobilize deal-focused institutions until we had an actual deal in hand. Of course, to get a deal in hand, you had to submit a bid, and to submit a bid, you had to have financial backing. F@&K.

Now, searching for an asset is easy. Like houses, they are constantly for sale. Unlike houses, the average citizen can't walk into a bank, get a pre-approval for a mortgage and then go buy a house. In fairness, we tried to do that. We were told we needed to have the house first.

Good learning. So, since we'd come this far in our goat-roping adventure of disaster, why not suspend the known principles of acquisitions and bid on an asset? We deserved a break, didn't we? This is how America was made: Hard work, determination, and a lucky break.

So, this dysfunctional team of ours found an asset, worked it up, pitched it to the board, and ultimately bid on it with the elusive "Conditional on Financing" in our letter. What this means in oil and gas terms is the following:

1. If it is a hot property, forget it.
2. If the bid is anywhere near what the asset is worth, forget it.
3. If there is any other bidder, forget it.

Our offer was rejected. We liked the asset even though it was a bit of a stretch for us financially, but it did provide some learning: We just needed to keep at it--our break was just around the corner.

By November, golf season was over, I was getting extremely impatient, and we were nine months in with a burn rate that had us done by January. I had one of my best friends move into the adjoining office because his kids were home during the day, and quite honestly, I was never there. I only kept it because of optics for Calgary. They were spending $15,000 a month on an office, what was $2,000? I might have gone into the office once a month. Maybe. Doubtful, but maybe.

Finally, I had used one of my contacts on a deal we had done at my previous company to get into an exclusive "pre-marketed" package. This means that instead of opening a giant auction, which scares people away, they call people, invite them to private meetings and then run a small auction, which is somehow a lot less scary. It's totally crazy to me how someone would reject Macaroni and Cheese but jump at the chance to eat Cheese and Macaroni.

A pre-marketed deal would give us a chance. From our 200-page pitch book and with a pre-marketed deal, we were finally able to get some good progress with an institution who said they could write a $100 million check and bring their friends who could write equally large checks. Hallelujah! We had done it!!!

We worked our asses off. I got to know the asset unbelievably well, put together development plans, rebuilt strategies, met with investors, got traction and then came the big moment.

I thought that the big moment was when we would get to have our very own closing dinner--the dinner where the bankers, the sellers, the lawyers and the buyers all sit down at a very expensive restaurant to tell each other how brilliant they are, how the greatest deal that could ever be put together has just been invoked, and how no wrong could ever come from the acquisition.

The big moment, as it turned out, hit when I got home from the airport. To get official exclusivity, we needed a deposit and a guarantee of our purchase price. To get a deposit from our investors, we needed exclusivity. To get our investors to go through investment committee where they would get approval to write a big check, they needed a U.S. private equity firm who knew the oil and gas space in the U.S. to co-invest with them. And to do that would take six to eight weeks, minimum. During which time, no one would pay a deposit, the deal would die, and we were back where we started, only with significantly less money in the bank, the same burn rate, and now a sense of impending doom like never before.

F@&K!!!!!!!!

Lesson Nine

What You Need to Know about Money and The Ligers

As a younger man, when I had spoken of Private Equity, or PEs as they are more commonly known, I would reflect, almost whimsically, on the great things about PE guys. Smart, hungry, young people with unending energy. They are tireless workers, literally pulling endless all-nighters for some artificial deadline that wears the tires right off them. You can always identify someone in PE because they look much older than you even when they are half your age, as most of them probably are.

When a Private Equity firm invests in a business, their goal and primary concern is to exit (or sell) at the highest price possible. This makes them easy to understand when you are the buyer and as a result of the frequent transactions they execute, they are incredibly savvy and know how to do deals. However, when you are with PE as a partner at one of their companies, it is far less romantic (which assumes the last two paragraphs sounded romantic to you…and, if so, you should immediately go buy your loved one a gift and apologize for your behavior. As a man, the good news is I never know what I'm apologizing for, so I just make it a habit to apologize in general for all the wrongs I have done this week).

Meeting the PE folks on their terms was what ultimately caused the deal we almost had to fail. What was worse was than the failing of the deal was the realization that our *flawed* business model would soon be a *failed* business model. I can explain this very simply: It was destined to be a failed business model because we didn't understand "The Money."

"The Money" and the people who control it, are the by far the most important factor when you are starting a business, growing a business, or running a business. They--your investors--control you. It is the true Golden Rule: He who has the gold, makes the rules.

Now I'm not saying that there is anything inherently wrong with that. Without money, no idea can take off and no business can be born. Therefore, it is the money and not the idea that takes first place. Ergo, if you don't know what "The Money" wants and how "The Money" works, you are F@&KED.

Having done a number of deals and been an active student of the markets and of the financial world, I truly thought I understood how the capital markets worked before we started StartUpCo. After having spent eighteen months living and dying by their every whim, I now know that I did not. I now know what our extremely experienced and well-respected former public company CFO with forty years of experience and now-CEO did not; the professors in my MBA did not teach me about it and I can only imagine they didn't really know about it either.

So I learned by doing, and while extremely valuable, it was the most painful lesson of all: For without the ability to raise money to fund our ideas, we were unable to have a viable business--a business for which we had raised $2.4 million dollars of our friends and families money to found (the original founders put an additional $800,000 in to extend the business after my original 30% ownership conversation with Michael). Perhaps I am overemphasizing the importance of "The Money", but I have 2.4 million reasons to believe what I say to be true.

Not understanding "The Money" was what led to StartUpCo's November turning point (also known as collision with iceberg). We had a deal in-hand that fit beautifully with the original strategy; we were in relatively exclusive negotiations with the vendor and in the last stages of fund raising. The term "last stages" in fund raising is relative – until the money is in the bank, you are in the "last stages."

Remember our simple business plan? Raise $500 million from institutions, the same institutions that invest in public companies, like Exxon Mobil and Apple? These companies have valuations that are in excess of what a private buyer would pay for similar assets. This is because public markets have lower rate of return thresholds than institutional and private investors. Can you imagine if I told you that you could get a 10% rate of return for the next five years? Wow. Sign me up.

With lower rates of return thresholds, the "cost of capital" to public companies is lower than it is to private companies, who are backed by venture capital, private equity, or large money managers whose careers (and therefore earning potentials) are based on beating the hell out of a 10% rate of return. Introduce Private Equity.

I was once in an investor meeting where I suggested that the minimum rate of return, we expected (and we were extremely happy with) was 12%. He looked at me and said, "I don't take a shit for 12%."

Oh. That's expensive shit.

The part about the cost of capital, I learned about in business school. The needing a rate of return higher than 12% to go to the bathroom, I did not.

But I am jumping ahead. Let us take a step back and analyze the investment industry. When I say, "Investment Banker" (the best of which are private equity guys), what image do you conjure? While you may use different words, I think of a Liger (i.e. a cross between a lion and a tiger, of *Napoleon Dynamite* fame--big mane, very fast, who has earned his stripes and wants to eat you).

They are almost always young, their career duration is extremely short, and the Ligers eat their weak (I don't know if this is true for Ligers, but like unicorns, they are an imaginary creation so I can take some license in describing their attributes).

The heads of firms--the Alpha Males--have all survived in the industry for an eon (so like ten years). They are scarred, they are proud, and they will eat you, the younger Liger, just for fun. So, when you pitch an idea to the Alpha Male, it had better be **F@&KING FLAWLESS**.

What makes a flawless idea? Well, it has to have been done before, be headed by someone who has done it before, and it has to be an absolute and complete shock to everyone if it doesn't work out. You may still be eaten, after all the Alpha's scars came from somewhere (no doubt a flawless idea) and being maimed by an Alpha Liger is not anyone's idea of a good time.

So, now you know the secret: Behind aggressive money--the money that is willing to take bets--there is an Alpha Liger and they are very, very scary. Though I did not know of their existence, I felt their presence and their demand for returns. Therefore, we built a business model to raise money from institutions which yielded lower returns, but also had lower risks. Nice, gentlemanly bankers who work from 9-5 and love to make 10%. They coach their kids' soccer, they make it home in time for dinner, and they most certainly will not eat you. Our model was built specifically with these fine fellows in mind: "Get funded, buy an asset that can deliver 10% cash on cash yield, and go public to capture the disparity in value between private assets (those held by PE guys basically) and public markets."

What we did not know at the time was that our gentlemanly bankers--and in retrospect, all institutional investors of the type--are structurally challenged. The most notable challenge is that their desire for return far exceeds the risk they are willing to take to achieve said returns. Moreover, they do not have the industry-specific expertise to invest in the opportunities that will give them their desired rate of return. For these reasons, these fine gentlemen almost always partner (and I dare say always partner) with a private equity firm. So, you take a business model such as StartUpCo's, you gear it towards the returns of institutions, and then you are introduced to a Liger… ROAR!

I have come to believe that PE firms were born of the need to link institutional money (who source these PE firms with huge amounts of money) to business managers in exchange for the Liger's share of the profits. And when a Liger gets involved, the hurdle rates (or required business plan rates of return) become those of the PE partner, not the bankers. The bankers get to go home for dinner just as the Liger is searching for prey.

Let's witness this in practice.

The Alpha-Male Liger picks up the phone or rather presses the speaker button because Ligers don't pick up phones, and calls an institution:

"Give us your money. We know what the F@&K we are doing."

The institutions say: "Okay." (They may be gentlemanly, but they are not stupid. So, when a Liger calls you and has a track record of making a lot of money and your bonus depends on how much money they can make for you, you comply).

With money in-hand after quickly being wired into a gigantic slush fund of "investment capacity" the Alpha Liger calls a meeting with the pride (or harem). All the adolescent ligers(lower case because they aren't an Alphas yet) take their position around the rock (which in most of these firms is a 130-foot marble conference table that was specially built in Italy and needed to be crane lifted through a window to make it into the building only to find that the table legs couldn't support the weight of the table so it remains unused until they can reinforce the legs and buy 120 chairs to surround the table for meetings that usually involve 4-6 people).

"Go find me some people who know what the F@&K they are doing…. And they better be F@&KING FLAWLESS."

The younger ligers, terrified that all their hard work could go to waste, race out of the conference room and search high and low to find management teams who look very similar to all the people their Alpha had invested in before (hopefully *were* the people they invested in before.)

To their new disciples who, like me, know nothing of the capital markets, the young ligers say:

"We will give you money, but you better know what the f@&k you are doing with it and your plan better be f@&king flawless." (In case you are wondering, young ligers don't speak in capitals.)

With that, management believes that money has fallen from the sky and given them the opportunity to run their own company and work for themselves. The love their newfound freedom; they love their jobs and they love their future fortune and fame that is just around the current. The Ligers and the lambs (also lowercase because you are always at risk of being eaten) can now go find things to spend money on. And when they do, the lambs invest their own money alongside the Ligers. Of the Ligers money (which is actually institutional money), the lambs return a "preferred return" --this is the return required to be paid ***before*** the management team makes any money. Let's say that the return is 10%. If you invest $100, after one years' time, you must return $110; two years, $121; three years $133; four years, $146.... TICK TICK TICK TICK.

When you finally sell at $200 in three years, you return the $133, you make $67 in profit, the lambs get 20% of that windfall, the institutions get their $133, and the Ligers feast on the excess-- almost $54 with very little risk (a four times multiple to what the management team gets lest you forget whether it is money or ideas that get the returns.) And they all live happily ever after.

Unless they don't. (Spoiler alert: It's when they don't, that things become drastically less fun.)

Ligers are very smart; they are very well funded, and they are surrounded by lambs. This is a very good model. The Liger gets ten lamb-filled companies and makes big bets with big risks in hopes that in a portfolio of ten companies, one fails (and the Liger responsible is eaten), one or two is a HUGE homerun, and the other seven or eight "flawless ideas" make a 10% return (despite the fact that they were supposed to be homeruns.) Just as they taught in business school, a portfolio-approach is most efficient when looking for returns.

The game is that the PE firm has already diversified its portfolio through concentration of each of its portfolio companies. They want everyone to succeed. But they know they won't, especially since the oil and gas industry is cyclical and it rotates in and out of basins. Public companies know this—just look at Exxon, Anadarko, Devon, and EOG. EnCana's split into pure play gas and pure play oil, however, has been a disaster.

Returns are related to risk. THAT they did teach us in business school. So, it stands to reason that as the hurdle rates increase, the risk and timing of the investment gets higher and earlier respectively. Higher risk needs higher specialization and this, in aggregate, self-selects management teams with basin-specific expertise. To quote a PE friend of mine, "I like to know that the team has been licking the rocks for the last thirty years."

The portfolio companies, or PCs as they are called, are all filled with basin experts who are ready to react to the opportunities in their respective areas which have great return potential. If you are a XYZ basin team and you see an opportunity in 123 basin…. "Why are you looking in 123 basin?!? What the F@&K is wrong with you?! Go back to looking in XYZ basin… we have 123 basin covered. I swear to God, next time I am going to eat you."

For the lambs, some are extremely successful: They find the right play at the right time and they make an insane amount of money, risk adjusted. For others, their concept doesn't work, the lamb company gets sold, the team goes in the penalty box, and the liger responsible gets eaten (so in this case, it's better to be a lamb.)

The worst scenario is what I call Private Equity Purgatory. This is a scenario in which you hope those that have crossed you end up. It is a horrible place and is truly the worst imaginable punishment. You, said lamb, have funding, have hired thirty of your closest business associates, have the perfect team, and have bought a deal that you need to invest capital into to prove it's the most incredibly flawless idea of your generation. Then something happens--perhaps the first few wells don't turn out as you planned, or the commodity price turns against you. The Ligers, in fear for the damage to their portfolio, cut you off. They no longer approve of any more investing, they know if they sell you now that they will have to mark down their investment and, in return, will be eaten, so they keep you. With no funding. While your interest rate clock ticks.... You can hear it, like the alligator in *Captain Hook*. Every day that goes on is a day in which your demand return gets higher making it less and less likely that you will get any money. But you can't leave. Oh, no. You are stuck having to go to work every day while smiling at your business associates and telling them that money is right around the corner. Then you go to your big office with nothing to do, nowhere to go, and no way out. THAT is Private Equity Purgatory.

We desperately wanted to avoid this fate, although, in fairness, we didn't know exactly what we were trying to avoid. The Ligers got involved, our "Last Stage of Fund Raising" became a "You Will Never Raise Money for This Model Stage of Fund Raising" and our November deal fell apart.

How can I summarize the learnings, without using the Liger analogy?

1) Institutional investors don't invest directly in industry unless they have expertise.
2) Those with expertise work at PE firms where they make A LOT of money
3) If you don't understand how PE/Venture capital works, you will be eaten (Liger or not)

Not knowing this, we had put a team together based on large-company experience and large-company capability trying to attract institutional dollars. None of us had ever been involved in a startup; none of us were considered a "basin expert"; and, worst of all, our structure was not based on the PE model of compensation (i.e. What you put in, you get out), but rather on equality of partnership. You know what a Liger says about equality? "What the F@&K is wrong with you? Are you some sort of special kind of special? Get the F@&K out of my office."

On December 31st, we laid off or parted ways with everyone except the two people who had invested the most money. It was our own special kind of Purgatory. Not as painful, but equally hopeless.

There is nothing wrong with Ligers, you just have to know how to tame them (because if you don't, it's lambs to slaughter).

Lesson Ten

If You Have to Pick Up the Phone More Than Once to Raise Money, You Shouldn't Be Raising Money

There is a case to be made that this chapter needs no further explanation. I have learned a lot over the last eighteen months: About companies, about cultures, about building a business, about the people you partner with and the people from whom you raise money. And while in every interaction there is something to be learned, I can honestly say this is the one you should remember.

I have had glimpses into this at times, but I missed the bigger picture. When we raised the $2.4 million dollars to start StartUpCo, I believed in what we were doing. It's why I so earnestly raised money from my family and my closest friends. But the business plan we wrote didn't require $2.4 million dollars. It required $500 million dollars and the people who were providing the $2.4 million couldn't close the gap. That was our biggest error.

I also didn't realize that the finance world is really about fees-fees for raising money, fees for advising, and fees for doing deals.

There is a cost of partnership, even amongst our first investors. That they believed in us (and in my case, me) is what led them to write the check, but they also assumed they would be compensated for the risk with an appropriate return.

When you are dealing with hundreds of millions of dollars and the people who run that money, and generate their income off the returns they get, there are no free lunches. You must be a known quantity; a known commodity; the closest thing to a sure bet you can get. There are many ways to be a sure bet but, in the oil and gas industry (where the price of entry is far above what most individuals can fund), but there is only one that really matters--a track record. This is extremely important.

When you go to an interview for a job, the interview process usually involves your resume which lists all your accomplishments in infinite positive detail if you don't know the company. If you do know the company and the person hiring you, then you don't need a resume. In fact, often, they call you and ask if you want the job. They know you will deliver the goods, and, in most cases, those types of partnerships will continue for many years.

Raising money is the same type of thing. It's so simple that I feel a bit silly for not realizing it sooner. If someone believes that you have what it takes, they will call you. End of story. If you are worth hearing about, then you have been heard about. You don't need to do presentations and PowerPoints to prove that you are capable. They are useful props to be sure, but I have been to a lot of money meetings and the only one that I have been a part of that was successful did not involve a PowerPoint. It also didn't involve a business plan. It was a meeting at a kitchen table (a very nice kitchen table, I will say) and we, the team (that wasn't even officially a team yet) described what we were going to do.

Our investors had invested in my now partner, friend and mentor, twenty years ago when he started his business from nothing, and he made them money. Then he kept making them money. And they kept calling him to put more money into him.

We reached an agreement for the first fund at $40 million, which was our request and much smaller than their desire. When we closed the fund, it was $50 million. A month later, they called because they had received investment board approval for $250 million. We didn't ask. We didn't even have a deal to spend it on. They called and said "Good news. You are funded to $300 million. Have a nice day."

If you have to pick up the phone more than once to raise money, you shouldn't be raising money.

[This is one of the most frequent and controversial pieces of advice I have given entrepreneurs since 2013 and I'll acknowledge that is some nuance to it. In order to be a successful capital raiser, I believe you need to have the people in your network TODAY to successfully raise capital from them. It could be for a real estate deal you have- the likely people who are going to put money in are the ones that know you, trust you, and believe in you.

In having an active network, you should also know the people that likely won't put money into 'this particular' venture- maybe it's not a focus area for them, maybe they are already fully deployed.

Whatever the case, my point is: when you make a call to someone, you should already know the answer because they are the right fit for the capital at the right time.

What I know for sure is that I have successfully raised capital as part of three teams and in each case, we made one phone call.]

Lesson Twelve

(Yes, we skipped Chapter 11)

Starting a Business You Write a "How Not To" Book About

I did not have this money-raising knowledge eighteen months ago when I was part of launching the first startup I attempted.

When we started our company, I was not a "founding" partner at the time. This may sound strange. How can you start a company when you weren't there to start a company? That's an excellent question.

It is important to know. And, similar to being fired, they don't tell you this in business school. I have a secret for you: A startup is not a real company.

It's sexy and glamorous and mysterious and fun. But it isn't a real company. It is a group of people working at something.

There are no mission statements. (Side bar: When companies have a mission statement that says, "We value our people above all else", they actually don't.... you don't need to say stuff like that if it's true).

There is no payroll, which doesn't always equate to no salaries; there is no one else to pay the bills, set up the office, or do the work. But there is always a plan. And most plans of the business variety fail.

The company is the collection of people that are part of it when you join. That much is certain. As a result, if a company doesn't have a product, a revenue stream, and you aren't pulling a conventional salary, you are a founder. You may not think you are, but I encourage you to change your mind on that. If you invested capital to start the business, you are a founder. I hope it helps bring others a clarity that I didn't have.

That is how you become a founding partner. You are one the moment you put money into it.

The business plan I wrote during the first interview almost a year before said "Find a small, easy, unloved asset that you can buy for cheap. Hire the staff you need, then grow into the $500 million." I knew it was the right plan at the time, but I ignored it.

Now, there is no right plan. I truly believe business plans are a waste of time. You know what you do well, so instead of writing about it, go do it.

I made a lot of mistakes in the first ten months by not trusting my gut, and by following my instincts, I would have had faith in the path. The things that dawned on me at the time—things that turned out to be extremely important—were buried in the interest of being politically correct. I wouldn't do it again, and I suggest you don't either.

Startups need entrepreneurs, not big company people. Big company people can be described as those who are very deep in specific areas, and, quite frankly, have "had jobs" their whole lives. They haven't started anything, they haven't taken any risks, and by definition (or my instinct), they do not respond well to uncertainty. We had five people in our startup. We needed no more than two.

Salaries are stupid. Part 1. When you put your own money in behind a business, there is only one thing you can do that is incredibly stupid. Pay yourself a salary that incurs income tax. This is obvious, but not always apparent. When you put $1 in a business, and pay yourself $1 dollar in salary, you paid 40% to the government purely for the right. AND, if you, like 67% of the businesses that get started, fall victim to failure, you now have a capital loss to write-off against investment gains that you don't have because you invested the money in yourself.

Salaries are stupid. Part 2. You have no idea, really, how long it is going to take before you have revenue. In the ideal world, you have a product that you can invest in, market test, build, and start to sell. But if it takes off, one of the leading causes of failure in successful businesses is working capital deficiency. The revenue cycle lags the inventory cycle. The inventory cycle takes cash. So, being able to survive as long as possible with all your seed money intact is key. I think back to my painting business and, at the time, I remember that I thought I should have been one of the crew foremen for the first month to get things going well. I didn't know how to paint but I knew how to manage, and I could draw a salary from the job to offset mistakes I may have made estimating. The company, of course, told me that they wanted me selling--me selling made them money. Me working made me money. I should have painted; I would have made more money. Expect not to draw a salary if you want to improve your chances at success.

Expenses you don't need are right up there with salaries. Stupid: I got an office for $2,000 a month and stayed there for twelve months. With no one else to meet or with whom to work. My partners were in Canada and Louisiana and they all had offices, too. At one point, our burn rate for offices was $20,000/month. Right now, I AM the everyone else.... Work from home. Write it off against the income that your partner makes or the income that you will make eventually. Depreciate your house so that when you sell it, the loss you have from your failed business (67% of the time) can offset the gain you had on your house because of the depreciation. Don't waste money.

Plans are subject to change. Instantaneously. In a startup, every day is a new day. I find I wake up with unbridled enthusiasm and optimism that today is the day we will hit whichever milestone we need to hit to get to the next milestone and bring us that much closer to having a company, not a startup. By the end of the day, I am usually in the depths of despair, having gone in six different directions, none of which got me to one of my milestones. I have a nice dinner with the family. Drink wine. Go to bed. Repeat. Where we have started to have the most success in this journey is to just "do." Someone wants to meet you. You meet. Someone wants to make a suggestion. You consider it. If it comes to your mind and is consistent with the strategy of your company, you do it.

If you are doing a startup, you are doing it for a reason. Sure, the money could be great as could the ego boost of being successful on your own. Both would be wonderful. But you are doing it because it's in your DNA.

I remember when I was twenty-five, just a few years out of school, and working at a large U.S. Independent oil and gas company. One of my classmates and friends was working at the largest oil and gas company in the world doing his rotation-in-training—a process which takes around ten years and weeds out all of the "everybody else" and leaves them with as much of the "sames" as they can. One mistake by that company, and they lose $100s of billions…. See Macondo for an example. As part of his training, my friend was placed in the marketing department and put in charge of selling the natural gas liquids for the company in Canada, which amounted to approximately $40 million of revenue per month.

Because of the IT protocols, the data system which housed the pricing information that the rest of the world got to use to find out what they should sell product for was not allowed on the server for this particular company. There is so much wrong with this story already--an engineer with no background, three years out of school, was selling a product he knew nothing about, with no system to understand the pricing.

Now, the good news is the protocols they have in place to make these sales mean it is impossible to mess it up. Or have success. You just do it. Every day. Exactly the same as the guy before you did it and exactly the same as the guy who will take your job when you go to the next cycle.

We were discussing this at lunch and my friend is a smart guy, so he finds this odd. He hasn't been there ten years and so they haven't weeded out his creativity yet (they have now…) He says to me, "It's so weird that I don't have this system. I could make about $400,000 a month more by knowing what the prices are… All these guys call me first and make me an offer because they know I don't know what the market is doing. The only thing that keeps them honest is they all know that I don't know, so they are reasonable about what they offer me because eventually I will see the data that shows me how much they make off of me." (This is their "system" that has worked for decades).

I said "Why don't you drill a hole in the office and bring in a separate cable entirely off the network to a computer (this was before wireless was as common as it is now with hotspots on cell phones) that gives you the data… for a couple hundred bucks a month, you could close the gap on the $400,000 and stay in compliance… you will be a hero!" I was excited! This was the first I had heard of this problem and I had solved it! His answer "And that's why you don't work here." Oh.

Use your creativity. When you have no resources, you have to be willing to do things and try things that everyone else hasn't, won't, or can't. In our present deal (which at this moment I give a 67% chance of being successful and closing and a 33% chance of not being successful and leading to us shutting the company down within weeks) we have no money, no resources, no people, no systems, processes, nor the ability to get any of that. Yet we have exclusivity on a $300 million deal being sold by a large public U.S. energy company.

We go to meetings (and when I say "we", it's me… my partner is in Canada and is a finance guy, not a technical operations guy), the company rolls out the twenty people who work on this asset every day to tell us (me) what is going on. I feel like I am riding a bull most of the time- I have no expertise in any of the areas they are discussing, but I've been around long enough and managed big enough projects that at least I've heard all the details at some point or another. The point is not to impress anyone. It's ridiculous. Conventional wisdom, which in this case is just wisdom of any kind, says we should not be in the room.

When we meet with financial partners and they say "who is the expert that you have looking at this deal?" The answer is no one. All we have is me. That really turns them off. First, I can't fund this deal (Ligers) with just you. Second. How do you know you are right? Third. You are crazy. And yet, if the deal is a good deal, and you know just enough to put the pieces together, it seems to work.

In this case, the creativity required was to find a deal that no one else could buy (think Dell's privatization) which, with no money, would still allow you to evaluate it and bid on it extremely conditionally. If the vendor is compelled enough to sell something that won't attract any bidders (and if it's obvious to the outside, it's only slightly less obvious internally), then they will be willing to work with you and give you exclusivity. With exclusivity, you can go to financial partners and convince them that it's a good deal. Assuming they agree that it's a good deal, they will devote resources to write a check.

And voila! Your partners are now the guys doing the due diligence. The better the deal, the keener they are and the faster it closes. The worse the deal becomes through the due diligence, the more scared they get. The more scared they are, the more reluctant the vendor becomes. Then, at the end, the vendor becomes your partner, and you are the savior to take the asset they really needed to sell off their hands because, literally, NO ONE ELSE IN THE WORLD can or will. This is ***SO*** far divergent from the original business plan, it's absolutely laughable. I'm going to start a charter school for homeless kids. Nope, it's a brothel. Oops.

What do all these musings mean? It all makes sense to me. Piece by piece, the plan has come together like a mosaic. And the more it came together, the tighter the plan became, but not because we started there.

It's kind of like this book. When I sat down to write it, I had no idea what a process it would be. You constantly have to think and rework the key themes--parts that were at the end of the book are now at the beginning, bits get cut, and lots of new stuff emerges. I've never been a fan of letting ideas marinate, and I'm not patient enough to do it anyway.

But I have learned through this book, this company, and the last eighteen months, that no matter how smart you are--or think you are--that you will not be able to predict all the twists and turns in ventures, in books, and ultimately in life.

You didn't know you were going to meet your husband or wife the day you met them, you didn't know you were going to be married to them at the onset of your relationship, and you don't know where things will end up. Hindsight is 20/20 and you do your best to learn, to predict and to grow, but I'm telling you, you really have no idea. You aim the car in the best direction you can, and you drive. That's all we can hope for.

[In 2015, I'd been working for 15 years and as a result of the downturn and for the first time in my career, I felt scared and needed income. I applied to be an associate professor at a University (no response), as a management consultant (thank you for your application) and a VP of Business Development (received word 2 years later in a PFO letter that I didn't have the experience). So I consulted to whoever I could. Had Uber been what it is now, I would have managed the 10 pm – 4 am crowd.

I reconnected with someone I had met in 2012 who had a vision; that vision led us to beg a friend of mine I had met in 2013 to join us. In 2016, we co-founded a company and the rest is history.

Your career isn't a ladder, it's a river. And some parts are fast and some parts are bumpy. But if you stay in long enough and make the most of every bend, things will work out.

#hottakeoftheday, September 2019]

Lesson Thirteen

Building a Team from Everybody Else

My research has shown that you cannot clone yourself. I have tried - many times. I quite like myself. Even on days when I don't, I'd still rather work with me or people very much like me than most anybody else, so cloning seemed like a real potential coup. Tried. Not possible. Check.

This fact is particularly relevant when it comes to the people you hire and worse, the people that your boss chooses to put you with. It is a sad reality that to have a team of any size, your hiring pool is everybody else. Fortunately for us, in most of the models of personalities, there are four quadrants in which everybody fits. Conveniently, this means that there are approximately 25% of "everybody's" similar to you. So, while you might not be able to clone yourself, you can have the next best thing.

Having been at a huge company, a medium-sized company, and a startup-acting-like-a-real-company, the question I have been known to philosophically assess is "Is it better to have a team of like yous or a team of everybodys?"

From an academic standpoint (and certainly from the MBA standpoint) the answer is most certainly "It depends."

From a conventional wisdom standpoint, I think the consensus would be that you need a well-rounded team of everybodys. Balance; symmetry; total dysfunction.

This may be intuitively obvious. But to me, it wasn't.

When I first got to BakkenCo, I had a team of Bs and Cs. That was my initial assessment and though I made changes to my team, the Bs and Cs just never left- either from my organization or my manager peers' organizations. BakkenCo had bought a U.S. based company that came with virtually no staff four years prior to gain foothold into the U.S. oil and gas industry. The market was hot, BakkenCo had no presence in Denver, and they hired who they could. When you hire who you can, you get warm bodies and eventually, bums in seats are no longer the objective. So, they looked to shake up the organization and they brought in two people- first my soon-to-be-boss Fred, who was in charge of the U.S. division and then second, shortly after him, was me.

At first, it was a dream job. I was leaving Anadarko because, with my champions gone, I was going no higher in the organization for a long time. I was ready to take the next step in broad organizational leadership instead of the narrower technical manager role I had at Anadarko and since BakkenCo was a Canadian company, I felt the job had been made for me.

Having been born in New York, a competitive athlete, and a type-A engineer, I was always too brash for a Canadian (and admittedly had a hard time when I lived in Canada). Although the two countries are similar, when I moved to the U.S., I found the differences striking. Had I moved to Algeria; I would have expected it. But I had assumed (incorrectly) the U.S. to be almost identical. It was not. And amazingly, it is the differences between the two countries that made me feel as though I was best suited to be in a Canadian company helping lead the U.S. offices.

The truth is people like working for people who are similar to themselves. The more alike, the better. If you are from Texas, or went to Texas A&M, you want that. If you can't have that, an American will do. Once you start going foreign, cultural differences start to creep in and misunderstandings grow.

I have a lot of theories and observations having been an American-born Canadian; a dual citizen who lives in America. The biggest difference, the one that drives everything else, is: Public health care.

In Canada, if you get fired, the first thought that goes through your mind is not "What happens to my health care?" In fact, that thought never crosses your mind.

Everyone talks about the Canadian health care system as being bad. Bad is relative. I think it's great and I lived there most of my life and my entire family lives there. Both of my children were born there, and I had my knee repaired there while I was still playing professional squash. It works.

Now, conversely, if you are having elective surgery, it will take a long time to get. But, if you have an emergency, like my father-in-law did when he broke his hip the day my second son was born, you get into surgery that day and wake up in the same hospital as your new grandson. They started walking at about the same time, too.

But this is not a debate about health care. It is a comment about when you need a job in order to have access to affordable health care, you stay a lot longer than you should. You don't retire, you don't change jobs. You get to the age where you know realistically you are limited in where you can go and are terrified of what will happen to your health care. So, you stay.

And when you stay, your sole goal is to stay employed. You do not rock the boat, you resist change, and you make it very hard for the company to get rid of you. Lawyers love discrimination lawsuits. They play badly in the court of public opinion and so large U.S. corporations are the U.S. answer to public health care, in my humble opinion.

I was not as aware of my assertion then as I am now. Five of the eight people who worked for me when I started were over sixty. Change was not a welcomed event; in fact, it was feared. With change comes new roles, new clarity, and the possibility of having to move on.

Being a change agent and an avid reader of airport business books, I know lots of "tricks":

1) You have 100 days before you become a part of the fabric of the new role or new company. Listening to people will help you discover the changes that are needed and how to enact them. Executing the changes when people are expecting it and before they get comfortable with the new pattern is when you have the greatest ability to do it.
2) You need a catalyst. Something people can see and point to that signifies the change.
3) You need a fly wheel of momentum. Once you get it turning, it's very hard to stop. Getting it going is the hard part.

For me, my first 100 days at BakkenCo had lots of executing but not enough listening- or rather too selective listening. My first change set the stage for what I now realize was a too drastic deviation from the norm.

As I'm sure is the case at many companies, working the front desk and answering phones is a huge deal. I don't truly understand the symbolism of it, but I suspect it has to do with the fact that:

a) It has historically been a woman's role in the workplace
b) That many people have started there and worked extremely hard to "get off the desk."
c) It is one of the most public roles in the company--everyone coming to the office sees you and therefore makes a first impression.

It should have been a cultural red flag but one of the biggest issues BakkenCo had (or thought they had) was that the operations team (my new team) would not man the reception desk. As a result, it was rotated amongst the accounting and land administrative staff, and this was causing huge friction (really?)

I was coming in to run the operations at the time, and of all the issues that were raised on day one, was the front desk.

One hundred days, catalyst, fly wheel. Check.

I called a meeting with my new staff, none of whom I knew, and all but three were significantly older than me—at least double my age on average. They wanted to go to lunch to welcome me. Alternatively, I had sandwiches brought in to show that saving money, even small amounts of money, mattered.

This was a bad decision. People want to go to lunch on the company. And they rarely get to. For less than $400, I could have made eight people happy. I saved maybe $300. It was stupid and I regret it. It didn't set the right tone. It put people on edge, and it made it harder for me to gain their trust. I was trying to watch the pennies while stepping over dollars. Bad investment.

So, with my cost efficiency plan launched, I decided it was time to address the front desk. I called a meeting with the operations "administrative" staff. All women, three of whom were over sixty. Two of the women were twenty-three year olds who had previously been "promoted" off the desk at other companies or left previous companies to pursue other opportunities not involving the front desk.

"Okay, so the other groups sit at the front desk. I would like a recommendation from you guys as to how we can pitch in."

Blank stares.

"It's important that we show the rest of the organization that we are a team. If windows need washing, we'll wash windows. We help. That's what we do. Isn't it great to be part of a team?"

Blank stares.

"Okay, how about I leave, you guys talk amongst yourselves, and come back with a proposal?"

A week later, we had the follow-up meeting, which I had set up the moment I walked out of the conference room. I was serious, I followed up. I was demonstrating leadership!

"So, how did the last week go? What do you have for me?"

Blank stares.

"Um, David. We didn't really talk about it. We think it's stupid that someone should sit at the front desk at lunch. We all have lunch plans and we don't want to do it."

Wrong answer.

"Fair enough, but we (the company) have decided it's important to have someone there. So, starting tomorrow, we will take the front desk on Tuesdays, starting with me."

Blank stares, but with much wider eyes this time.

"You can't do that."

"Actually, yes I can. It's fair and it's not a big deal."

So, I did it. Never having had sat at the front desk or answered phones or welcomed people in my career, but I did it that day. I took calls from angry people, bored people, and had extremely rude salesmen trying to see the senior guy. Would they wait? Yes.

One o'clock came and I stood up from the desk, walked over to the salesman and said, "I'm David, I believe you were trying to meet with me?"

Blank stare.

I understand now why people don't like the front desk and I'm really glad I did it. I made enemies with my team members because I didn't understand their issues--some of them gender specific--and sitting at the desk only made it worse to them.

At the company I start, people will work the front desk because it's important. Just as they will put together furniture, make reservations, negotiate deals, and celebrate success. Because those are important jobs. Eventually, you need specialists, but until you do, everyone should pitch in and be happy to do it.

Cultures don't change. The people you hire are the culture you have. Hire the right people.

Also, I strongly believe size matters. Large companies need a balance of people to even out the multiple dynamics. Great leaders get the most out of the staff they have. The company culture doesn't shift. Eventually a big shake up, merger or restructuring leads to change or the company dies.

Entrepreneurs are everywhere, at all ages and levels in varying sizes of organizations. Large companies need them for catalysts. They create huge amounts of value, get promoted and, more likely than not, eventually outgrow the organization and leave.

At small companies, I think you need like-minded people. And those like-minded people are initiative takers. The great leaders harness their energy, put it to useful work, and they create a company. Eventually, the entrepreneurs decide they want to do it for themselves and go start their own companies, hire their own people, and the cycle repeats.

I think the key to successful hiring is understanding where you are, what you need, and managing the ramifications that are created from doing so. If you are going to start a company, I strongly recommend you get people that you have worked with before in stressful situations. If that's not a viable option, find people that are like you—doers—and know what you are trying to accomplish.

Perhaps more than anything, companies are about fit, and unlike 20 years ago, and perhaps even 10 years ago, the contract between employer and employee has changed and it's important to recognize the change.

Can you imagine dating someone twice and then deciding to get married? The first date is just to get to know them over the course of an hour; ask questions of each other and decide if it's worth going to the next step. The second date is time to meet the family. After that, you decide this is a good match, you propose, and you are married. Happily, ever after.

That's the way the interview process works. And more often than not, we start at the new job, we get ninety days in (sometimes we get one day in) and we say "What the F@&K is wrong with all these people? This place is horrible!" But we stay. Sometimes, we work through it. Most times we don't.

Your job occupies at least forty hours a week of your time and drives much of your mood and most of your income. It is a contract between a product or service provider who needs your talent and you. They get value, you get paid and the fulcrum is culture. If you don't deliver, the scale tips one way. If you aren't valued (money, days off, four days per week…whatever it is you value), it tips the other. But the thing that makes buffers or amplifies the imbalance is the culture. Don't be afraid to say, "This relationship isn't working for me." When the relationship is working, the grass isn't always greener. In fact, it's probably just spray-painted during the interview.

When you are going to a new company, think of it as dating and really try to find the right one when you move. Talk to employees before you accept the job; spend more than three interviews and think more about the base salary they are going to give you because once you get in, you will get the same raises you have for years and you have to live with marriage, not courting.

I am not suggesting anything earth-shattering and I am not trying to collapse the establishment. I think that the contract today is better than it was when it was cradle-to-grave. The seat belt sign is off, and people are free to move about the cabin, to move cities, to change opportunities, to seek out the perfect balance. That should lead to more freedom and greater contentment in a large part of your life.

I have found entirely by accident that consulting is a great way to date. You see a lot of companies from the inside--you give value, you get paid, and you understand how the fulcrum is made. It's pretty eye-opening. I've had six or so consulting engagements over the last year (all simultaneously) and I've found good things about all of them. But I've also seen the culture, and over time, I'm confident I would have been frustrated at five of them. As it so happens, with consulting, the value and the service was balanced and it never caused me stress, which made me happy and fit, which makes me a better person today.

[Related, the oil and gas industry is going through and will continue to go through a substantial wave of consolidation. I believe that ultimately there will be 10 or so mega companies in 3-5 years and everyone else will be private (as in not publicly traded). In saying this, and as G&A is cut as part of the "cost savings", the unfortunate thing is many in the acquired company will be let go- it is not their fault, it's just related to this "culture thing".

***

Business school professors might tell you that in an acquisition, you should take the best of both companies and make the Newco "better". That's why I wrote the book – "…What They Didn't Teach You in Business School". Most people teaching have never been through an acquisition personally and just interviewed some CEO 10 years after the fact for a paper they wrote and think they understand corporate culture. They do not.

The people that work at OXY and CVX do so because they like it; they fit the culture; and they understand the politics. If they didn't, they would leave or be forced out. From what I know of those cultures – I would be a horrible fit and they would be best to be rid of me ASAP. I did work at APC for a long time and I would say generally I was a good fit. So. Post merger – OXY and CVX would have to get rid of me and all the "like mes" to keep us from rocking the culture boat. And how would they know who those people are? They don't but they can't make a mistake.

That's why they must get rid of almost everyone and post every job they need while inviting applications from EVERYONE to find people who will fit at best OXY or CVX. Because a warm body WILL NOT do when there are so many people available.

#hottakeoftheday, May 4th, 2019]

Lesson Fourteen

You Pay Them What?

[Does anyone else find it ironic that some of Ray Dalio's biggest 'fans' are the least common followers of his core philosophy? Radical transparency. Well, it amuses me, so let's take the actual principle and talk Compensation ahead of year end reviews.

If compensation is truly linked to performance, why is it a social norm not to talk about your comp with your co-workers? Shouldn't they be able to look at your comp and say "yeah, I agree with it".

Think about the benefits. No more gender wage gap (it would be based on contribution); no more questioning "does my boss like me?" (It would be pretty clear if your peer makes 30% more and gets better bonuses) and most importantly, you would be able to have a two-way compensation conversation (Can you imagine??).

I've always been up for posting everyone's compensation and bonus targets in the kitchen - especially for new hires. Amazing what 'shining the light' does to clean up inequality. There is a reason the lights that come on at 2 am are called "the ugly lights".

#hottakeoftheday, December 7, 2019

It stands to reason that after being fired, one of the first things I did was put my compensation philosophy into words. I didn't know when, or if I would get to implement it but after having been seen the disparity in earnings amongst my staff and peers and having been unceremoniously dumped with a package that left much to be desired, I thought it was a worthwhile endeavor. Quite frankly, I'm not convinced the people who have been tasked with writing one for companies in the past have had any earthly idea what they were talking about.

When I was at University, long before I truly entered the workforce, I discovered that I could write the "final exam incentive". Engineering is an extremely heavy course load, and there are very few electives so it's hard to boost your GPA with that "*Music Appreciation*" class I heard so much about. But the students had a bail out: your final mark, the one that would show up on your transcript and last forever could be calculated from one of two sources: either the average of the entire year of performance or, to "reward" students for studying hard for the final, if the mark on the final was higher than the average for the year, that was the mark you got. So, being efficient and not particularly risk averse, I would pack the entire semester into three days and wrote the final. I bought myself 120 days of relative freedom and I achieved a respectable GPA. When the result generated is materially different than the intent of the incentive, that's a misalignment of incentives.

My first interaction with this in the business world was in 2003, when I was a young engineer at Anadarko. The company had decided to divestment one of its key and now "non-core" assets and I was fortunate enough to work on the team that was putting the lipstick on the pig. It was a cute pig, but all sale processes require lipstick in hopes of finding Daddy Warbucks who dramatically overpays for the asset they just bought from you. It's like staging your house for the showings or how at furniture stores, they demonstrate the sleek lines of the computers and electronics on the furniture and magically, none of them need unsightly wires or cabling.

Also on the project was my best work colleague-friend, which isn't a real word but research shows that job retention is highest when you have a best friend at work, and therefore people who stay at companies for long periods of time are more likely than not to have this person. For me, it was Heather. For weeks, we worked night and day at the office—often times until 2 a.m. Heather and I worked round-the-clock, lived for the job, and I couldn't have been happier. There were a lot of people on the project and a lot of hard work was put in; the asset was sold for a nice price and everyone was happy.

That is, until bonus time rolled around. This event was one of the most instructive business moments in my life, and one that I will credit as being the formative event in the development of my compensation philosophy. My reward was a $150 gift certificate to the best restaurant in town. I was thrilled! Mena, with whom we never talked about money, was also very happy, though I don't know what she got. Others were not.

Others felt they deserved heaps of cash for their efforts. After all, they were *working*, and *working* in the oil and gas industry is a bit odd at times. Salaries are for showing up, bonuses are expected for actually doing something and they are really viewed as base pay. Then, actually doing something worthy of a bonus means a bonus on top of the bonus.

That gift certificate as a reward for all my hard work was phenomenal. It didn't disappear into my bank account, so I remember exactly what I did with it.

My wife and I went to dinner and ordered a bottle of wine, because that's what grown-ups do. Grown-ups also have dessert. And an after-dinner port. But people pretending to be grown-ups go home and because they liked the port so much, they open up the bottle of port they got as a wedding gift. Since it was the first bottle of port they had ever opened, they mistakenly assumed it was like wine and didn't want it to spoil, so they drank the entire bottle that night. And woke up extremely hung-over and totally unable to function for remainder of the weekend. It was one of the best dinners we ever had, and I always remember the day the President of the company handed it to me and said, "Thank you for working so hard."

That's a bonus.

Since that moment, I have thought of bonuses differently. Base pay is base pay. If you expect a bonus, it is no longer a bonus. I would rather pay you your salary plus bonus every two weeks so that at the end of the two weeks, you can decide: I like it here, I want to stay, and not because I have money on the table. If you don't like it, you don't drag on for six months, hating your life and hurting the people around you. You pack your box and you go.

On the other hand, if you stop performing at the level that got you the salary and bonus in the first place, I also want you to go. I don't want to set a precedent with big severances and payment of bonuses unearned which only cause problems because I have done enough of that in my career already. I want to part ways with you, in a dignified, respectful, and fair way. I've paid you well, we've had many talks about your performance along the way, it isn't working out anymore, and it's time to go.

On the subject of going, that is another biggie. You should never be surprised that you are being let go. It should also not be subtle, and just "documenting" problems for HR to keep on record so that you can be fired at lower risk of a lawsuit. If you have a problem, talk to the person about it. Be precise about the shortcomings, give specific examples of where they can improve, set milestones and goals for them, and set a follow-up meeting right then.

These are actually not hard conversations to have. They are open, honest, and trustworthy. If someone doesn't like to receive feedback about their performance, they probably won't improve, and eventually, you won't want them on your team.

The best way to deal with this is open and up front. When you remove compensation from the equation, it comes down to the performance of the person and the relationship they have with you. You must retain people in more ways than just monetarily if you want them to be truly happy.

When someone was leaving the company of their own choice, I always asked "Why did you pick up the phone to leave?", not "Why are you leaving?" It's the picking up the phone part that I want to prevent. Once someone has made the decision to leave, it's time to leave. And the sooner and more pleasant, the better.

When I got fired, the thing that upset me the most was that I would have stayed for twelve weeks despite knowing that I was going to be out on my ass. I would have transitioned the team, the leadership, the expectations; I would have been a soldier. I would have looked for another job quietly, and I would have left with lots of warning, in a way that maximized the chances of the organization to be successful.

They could have put restrictions on everything, gag orders on things, and I would have done it happily every day. It shaped the way I feel, and I truly believe it's one of the best things that came out of being fired in the fashion that I was. I learned just how much a small action can make the world of difference when someone feels as if they have been treated fairly, or alternatively, unfairly.

It's also very important to tie back to how companies pay people. And this stems back to the power you have at a company. People who are in the same job are likely drastically differently paid, even if they do the exact same job. They usually have different vacation time and raises, and bonuses NEVER close the gap. People get hired at different times from different places and companies always have a range. I would be willing to bet you that there is someone in the exact same role as you that has double the vacation and 50% more pay. Unfortunately, companies have not been able to move away from compensation systems that weigh years of experience into role contribution.

What does this mean to you? If you look at your W2 at the end of the year, and you think about how much you made, and you think about everyone else in your position and what they made, there is 20-40% difference in my estimation. So, if you feel like you are being underpaid, you probably are. And if you are underpaid, you can pretty easily fix that. You can either change jobs or you can ask for a raise to bring you up to par with your peers. It's also possible (shockingly) that you are overpaid. It's that easy.

The job market has been tight for the last few years. I get that. But it costs 25-50% of a person's salary to replace someone, train them, and get them to your level. If you are good at what you do and you believe the company wants to keep you, they can, and they will. Ask.

If you want to go four days a week, ask.

If you want an extra week of vacation or want to "buy it" (spend 1/52 of your salary to buy an extra week), ask.

That said, if you are a mediocre performer, there is a good chance that your boss will say no and it will negatively impact your career.

But if you are someone who sits at your desk, looks at all the people who are around you, socializing, doing personal errands during work time, not working that hard, I promise you "the boss" knows it and they have chosen not to do anything about it. There are lots of reasons for this, and I will elaborate, but in this context what matters is you, not the boss.

Compensation matters. But not in the way people think. It's what you need to stay somewhere, not what makes you feel valued while you are there.

[Ah, compensation. I have been passionate about this topic for years but didn't necessarily appreciate where it came from. Obviously, the topic of this chapter is about the 98% who are employees, but in 2019, I am far more focused on the misalignment of Executive Compensation.

***

Let's talk about executive compensation- the touchy subject sure to offend people for the first time since I started my hottakes…

Oh, I've offended you previously? Good. It's like falling while skiing: if you're not offended, you aren't growing as a person. You're welcome.

*To me…and maybe I'm the only one- it is the sum of the parts- from the Pumper to the Manager and above- that in concert- run all the parts of a company. So why are the Cs often paid 40x more than the people doing the heavy lifting and are rarely fired when bad sh*t happens?*

Running a company is hard- for sure. But change of control $100 million hard?! $7 million per year to have meetings and play on your phone hard? No.

Me- if you were asking- I'd pay my top 5 in stock above the median salary of their managers and require that they personally own 5x their cash compensation in stock. Radical. Maybe. But if they don't get smart, it's going to be a huge election issue in 2020 and even most republicans would agree, executive compensation is out of control.

#hottakeoftheday, October 2019]

Lesson Fifteen

You Might Not Know It Yet, But It Will Work Out

Best friends are great, and I highly recommend them--especially when they are willing to give you great advice that no one else will. One of my closest friends, Chad, and I have known each other for seven years. Remember when I got transferred to the U.S. at the beginning of the spiral? As you may recall, I had departed from Canada gloating, had just started my MBA, and I was working in Denver while my family was living in Calgary.

I was commuting every Monday and Thursday, working from home on Fridays, in class all day Saturday, and then had "family time" on Sunday. "Family time" was usually spent doing assignments, planning for the week ahead in Denver, and Sunday dinner at my parent's house or my wife's parent's house.

The first question that comes to mind is "Why did I do this to my family?" With a one year old and a child on the way, it is easy to make the case that I was a selfish idiot. In fact, you don't even need to make the case; I was a selfish idiot.

In fairness, my role models were all about career as well, so it comes as no surprise that "sacrifices" were part of the expectation. Moving was just one of those sacrifices and I was willing to make it.

Would I make the same choice again?

When we look back on our own lives, we all want there to be no regrets. Mistakes we can live with; regrets we can't. Everybody says that, and we can even rationalize regrets as mistakes, but can we look deep inside ourselves and really decide between the two?

I used to have a regret: When I was recruited for University, I had the opportunity to go to Princeton to play squash. Of course, with my father who had retired with "enough" money, my family was going to have to foot the entire tuition bill at an Ivy League school—about $40,000 per year. Comparing that to The University in Calgary, which had one of the best engineering schools in the country and would cost only $3,000 per year, it was a no-brainer. Furthermore, I could also be easily recruited into the oil and gas industry—a career in which I had dreamt of working in since before I was sixteen.

So when my father asked "Where do you want to go?", my answer was memorably simple: "Give me the money and I'll educate myself."

I didn't get the money, but I didn't go to Princeton either. Life went on, as it tends to do in the wake of major decisions. My squash kept improving, I stayed in Calgary, I took the internship program, and eventually got hired into the industry for which I was destined to go.

Many of my squash playing friends who had gone to Princeton, Harvard, Yale and the like were starting their young careers as well. Only instead, they were investment bankers in New York, as everyone was becoming in 2001. "Oh, you have a B.A? Investment banker." "Engineer?" "Banker!?" "Political science major.... Investment banker!" I was where I had always wanted to be, but a niggle of doubt crept in...What if I had gone to Princeton instead?

Well, for starters, I wouldn't have met my wife. I wouldn't have stayed in Calgary. I wouldn't have done an internship that allowed me to get BD experience. And I wouldn't have been an engineer.

Flash forward five years. I was young, smart, and arrogant. I was really good at what I did precisely because I was an engineer who understood finance and who had been pushed with the expectation that I would someday run the company. I didn't go to Princeton and I didn't become an investment banker. But, still ever present, was that twinge of self-doubt – I would have been a great investment banker. So, when the call from a headhunter revealed that there was an analyst job open with an investment bank in Calgary, I answered the phone.

In my mind, investment bankers were pure meritocrats. This is a real thing. Reward based on merit. I know, it sounds mythical, but you can find the definition on Wikipedia (the source of all truth). In these cultures, you perform, or you die. No sleeping at meetings, no six-week vacations in the summer. No 3:30 p.m. crickets in the hallways. You were getting your morning coffee at 3:30 p.m. and just gearing up for a long night. It seemed like Heaven.

There were lots of other reasons I took the call, which is why I always ask the question when people leave. It's not "Why are you leaving?" It's "Why did you pick up the phone?" The company for whom I was currently working, Anadarko, was struggling to find its identity in Calgary. We weren't having great success with some of our assets, a lot of people were leaving, and a lot of people were unhappy. I always believed I would be a "lifer"; many of my friends had already left their first jobs and were into their second and third. It surprised almost everyone that I had lasted at a big company. It seems that they knew I was of the entrepreneurial ilk long before I did. But I doubt they appreciated the family influence and those two little phrases: Don't leave a big company until you understand why it needs bureaucracy and don't leave a company until someone taps you on the shoulder and says you are going no higher. I still believe those pieces of advice and give them to everyone I talk to when they are early in their career or looking for jobs.

In fact, when I left Anadarko and went to work for a much smaller company, I used to tell summer students on their first day of working for me that "No matter how good you are, I will not offer you a job at the end of the summer." It shocked them. It probably angered them. They are thinking "What the F@&K is wrong with this guy?"

The reason was simple: We were too small to give them the experience they needed to be extremely successful. I truly believe only a big company can do that and everyone should work for one early in their career. If they start in a small company, they will never be able to handle the processes of big companies. If you don't know the processes, you can never grow a small company to be a big company with you as the leader.

To the interns I said, "I want you to get a job at the biggest company you can, and after you know why you need bureaucracy and you aren't going any higher, call me. I'll be waiting." It freed them up to explore, to make mistakes, and to not think that they were on a four-month interview with me during their internship. I think it made them better then and I trust it makes them better now. I hope they read this book and agree. If they don't, I'd ask they put a note in the complaint jar outside my office, just above the shredder. Just kidding. I don't have a shredder. It's a garbage can.

I am proud of all the summer students I have mentored. I hope they remember me and believe that I have had a positive influence on their careers. They were great kids and I will hire them all when they call.

So, after five years at Anadarko, I went to my first interview for another job-- to be an analyst. Prior to the interview, I had written down a list of everything I would change at my current company, Anadarko, including why it wasn't the company it could be and all the reasons for which I was leaving. I slipped the note it in my pocket and brought it to the interview so that if they asked, "Why are you leaving?" I knew the answer.

They never asked and I forgot about the sheet of paper.

On my way back to the office, I stopped at Subway to get a sandwich to take to my desk. The president of Anadarko Canada, Mike, who eventually was responsible for my transfer to the U.S. and recommended that Anadarko pay for my MBA, happened to get into line directly behind me. At this point, I had only met him a couple of times previously.

"Hello, David."

"Hi, Mike, how are you?"

"Good, how are you?"

"You want the short answer or the long answer?"

"Let's start with the short."

He had no idea that I wanted to be an investment banker or that I had just gotten back from an interview- he just believed in talking to his people.

With that opening, I brought out the list of all the things I would change about Anadarko to make it better. In the line at a Subway in a food court. Yep, I did that.

After about three bullets, Mike said "Why don't you book a meeting with Holly tomorrow and you can walk me through the entire list."

Yep, he did that.

I went home elated. I converted my list into a PowerPoint presentation, and he gave me an hour and a half of his time while I walked him through what I, David Ramsden-Wood, would do to fix the company.

I didn't take the investment banking job. I instead got offered a supervisor role within Anadarko Canada with the opportunity to get a fully paid for MBA at any place of my choosing. And, subsequently, when Mike got offered the job to run the Denver office after the amazing merger that we had just executed and offered me a position, I told my wife I was going--with or without her.

My best work friend, Heather, was also given the same offer to move to Denver. But she had a young son at home, a husband who is extremely good at what he does in the energy industry as well and decided not to take the job. At the time, I thought she was absolutely crazy. Would I have made the sacrifice today, knowing what I know now? I'm not sure.

The week before I started in Denver, I was over the moon. I had a promotion to the leadership team at twenty-eight, the youngest by about ten years, and I needed to look the part. I went out and bought a $2,000 dollar suit, $400 shoes, $250 belt, $200 shirt, a $125 tie and $40 socks. Hugo Boss. I looked like $3,015 bucks. I showed up in Denver to my first leadership staff meeting and everyone was wearing golf shirts. Mike said, "Take that tie off, you don't need a suit here."

That sound you hear is the air rushing out of a balloon--a $3,015 balloon.

On my first business trip to Houston, I met Chad (colorful shorts Chad) Which, conveniently, is where I started this chapter--with best friends and why they are great. While I would like to say that our first meeting was at a football game discussing some fancy shorts and a guy impressing a girl, because that's an amusing story, I can't. I met him at the office trying to figure out how to spell his last name so I could find him in the corporate directory to get to his sixth-floor office. Chad was a high-flier like me; he had done all of the modeling on the deal and was one of the smartest and most thoughtful people I had met. We hit it off instantly, and we have been friends--and then best friends--ever since.

Unlike me, Chad is slightly less outspoken and a much better listener. He is instantly likeable, incredibly flexible, and, among his many other talents, fits in well at big companies. It is not to say he doesn't fit in elsewhere--he would be extremely successful at whatever he chooses to do. But one of his best talents is managing groups of people and big companies have groups of people that need to be led. As I write this, I know that he will be a CEO at a $25+ billion company if he so chooses. But, like me, he wonders, "What if?": What if I learn to hit a fade instead of a draw? Isn't the grass greener on the other side of the fairway? What if I leave to a smaller company and do what I enjoy slightly more?

To him, and to you, I would say: "You have been there for ten plus years. You fit. People like you. You've never been tapped on the shoulder. You may have to make five job changes before you find something half as good as this. Find the good, forget the bad, and do your best."

But he's never asked me that in a way that required an answer. So, I listen (surprisingly) and endeavor to be the best friend I can be to him.

He was that friend to me. Which, again, is why I believe so strongly in best friends. He is the one that led me to today. And every day since. And I am grateful.

In 2009, he was the one who gave me the tap on the shoulder and said "David, you aren't going any higher here, it's time to move on."

It was the best piece of advice I had ever had, and the reason that I am a big fan of best friends and strongly recommend them. He was also one of the first people to put money into StartUpCo and apologized that it wasn't more.

So when he came to Denver for Christmas in 2012, it should be no surprise that after seeing what happened after I got fired and the events that were transpiring at StartUpCo, Chad said "David, promise me you'll never work for anyone again. You're ready to start something yourself."

That was the day I started Prevail Energy. I started consulting to companies outside of StartUpCo as an insurance policy since I had no idea where or how long StartUpCo would last. I designed the logo myself and had a friend make it a reality. It is the statue of Atlas from behind carrying the world on his shoulders. It had to be from behind (no, that's not a fetish, stick with me, you are almost finished the book!) It is to say, "Follow me and we will get there." It had to say, "I'm happy to carry a heavy burden." It had to say, "I trust you to be behind me and I know you are taking care of things when I'm not looking."

It is my company and it is what I am most proud of in my career. I don't really know what it is, or what it will do, but it's mine. The logo means something to me. If I ever hire anyone, I know the compensation philosophy. I know the mission statement. I know the values. I know what we will do and what we will not do. And I know that the most important part of the equation is the people--the partners that I get to work with.

That's why when Bill called me to reconnect after our first meeting and needed help building a model, I was thrilled to get a chance to work with him. And to continue working with Michael. And do investor relations and strategy and finance and deal analysis, take my kids to school, work whenever I want, and be genuinely appreciated for my skills and my quirks. I'm the combination of an engineer, an investment banker, and an entrepreneur. Interesting.

And what did I do this time around?

Start small I have an office in the house, a single computer, my cell phone and a logo.

Don't plan Every day I wake up and I start working. I assess the balls in the air, I decide which one to catch, what to do with it, and throw it back in the air to be caught at some later date.

Don't compromise I know what I'm good at. I know what I'm not good at. I don't do what I'm not good at.

Be happy If I don't like the way something is going, I change it. If it's going well, I do more of it. If I'm frustrated, I go for a walk. The worst days now are better than most of the best days before.

I have my health, my family, my friends, and my happiness. Could I have gotten here without the sacrifice? I don't know. I hope you can. That's why I'm writing this book.

[In a return to the #hotquestionoftheweek, we will put off "The Beatings" series until Monday.

"It kills me to acknowledge that you're right in your pessimism. Instead of griping about how badly the industry is screwing up, can you offer some of us a solution? I'm in my 30s with all my experience in O&G- if I have no future in this industry, how do I get out? PS. You really don't know where apostrophes go, do you?"

2nd question first. No. I have no idea's. 1st question. Longer answer.

In 2015, after being fired for the 3rd time for sharing my hottake on my boss's opinion's, there weren't a lot of option's. I'd been working for 15 years and I needed income. I applied to be an associate prof at DU (no response), a mgmt consultant (thank you for your application) and BD (you don't have the experience). So I consulted to whoever I could. Had Uber been what it is now, I would have managed the 10 pm - 4 am crowd.

Consulting led me to reconnect with someone from 2012 with a vision; and that vision led us to beg a friend from a startup I did in 2013 to join us. We co-founded OneEnergy.

Your career isn't a ladder- It's a river. And some parts are fast, and some parts are bumpy. But if you stay in long enough and make the most of every bend, things will work out.

#hottakeoftheday, September 14, 2019]

Lesson Sixteen

The Right Person at the Right Time

As I write this, I'm sitting on a plane flying across the country for an investor meeting in New York, though it's not for me and it's not even for a company that I'm officially a part of. I am "the consultant." To us? For us? I don't know. StartUpCo is dead. We haven't closed the doors, and we are trying to keep it afloat, but I know it in my heart. You know it as you read this. And I started my consulting business and my first client is Bill, for whom I'm flying.

Our company- in fact, it's not a company at all--it's just three guys and a couple of computers (Hmmm, "Three Guys and a Couple of Computers?") and some investors who asked to see us. What few investor meetings I had done to date, this was NOT the way things usually went.

Timing is everything. I met Bill ten days after being fired and it was the first official meeting I had for StartUpCo. It was an interview.

The view was in order to go public (which you can tell from the lessons in this book was an absolute certainty!), you need to have a CEO who doesn't look like he was born yesterday, or even within the last thirty-five years, which ruled me out. Enter Bill. We met him through the same headhunter that I had used to get to StartUpCo.

Michael and Perry, StartUpCo's founding team, had loved him and they really wanted me to meet him. He would be "my boss," so it made sense that I should meet him. Plus, in Michael's mind, Bill "didn't get" our business plan and the assets (or cars) we were trying to buy. Since I "got" the plan, I might be able to explain it in a different way. I have since learned that if someone doesn't get your plan, it really just means they don't like your plan.

We met at a small restaurant in Houston. Just Bill and me. And Sandra.

Who the F@&K is Sandra? I had no idea.

"David, it's very nice to meet you. I'm Bill, and this is my wife Sandra."

Years before, my father-in-law, George, who was a very successful oil and gas executive but not a particularly funny guy, told me an absolute classic about a Vice President in his company who reported to him who had brought his wife to the annual review. I'm not kidding you. I couldn't make this up.

George sort of looked at him, and then looked at her, and said, "Um, is there something I can help you with?"

She responded, "Yes. I, well, WE feel that Brian isn't being promoted fast enough to really be able to meet his potential and that, quite frankly, you are using him on tasks below his skill set and he's not making it home for dinner. We need a raise, someone to work for him to get stuff done, and a promotion." I'm serious. This actually happened.

George said "I appreciate you coming down, but I'm going to have to ask you to leave so I can chat with your husband." She got up, left and closed the door behind her.

"I'll start looking for another job."

"Yes, that's a pretty good idea."

So, with this story front and center in my mind, I can tell you that I've never been to a business dinner in which I'm meeting someone for the first time who has brought his wife with him.

Before I went to the meeting, Michael had sent me Bill's resume. After recently polishing mine up and having gone through probably 5,000 other resumes in my life, Bill's was by far the most memorable. It was a single page. I remember it so clearly.

Bill

Objective: To create value for a company, start-up or spin-off by restructuring, refinancing, or rationalizing the assets.

Work Experience:

1996 – Present. Manage personal portfolio.

1982 – 1996. Started company. Took public. Became most active driller in the United States. Sold company for $500 million. Key investors: <Name Brand Guy>.

1979-1984. Real estate development. Key investors. <Large University> and Duchess of <XYZ>.

Education: Attended California prep school. USC and UC Boulder. No Degrees.

***

I kid you not. That was his resume. I'm not remembering only bits and pieces--that was it. And now I am meeting his wife at our first dinner. Who the F@&K is this guy? This is going to be a chapter in my book, for sure!

Dinner was awesome. Bill, Sandra, and I "clicked." The conversation was so easy and the three of us (which was weird at first) talked about the type of company we wanted to build, our experiences, our visions. We discussed the way the office would be laid out and the culture it should have. We talked about the company he had built and what it was like to sell it and leave and we talked really openly about my being fired and what I learned. We were candid, open, and it was a great four-hour dinner. At the core, Bill's philosophy was that he knew stuff that I didn't, and I was willing to do stuff he didn't want to do anymore. As a team, it would be extremely compelling.

The story of Bill is so great it's worth repeating.

In the 1980s, after coaching basketball and doing real estate, he started an oil and gas company. No experience. No college degree. And a first wife that didn't support him. He just did it.

I say, "started an oil and gas company." It was more like ended up with four wells in the middle of the state when he and his brother had a falling out. I don't know what possessed him to start buying more wells in an industry he really didn't understand or to live in an SUV while driving back and forth between wells and figuring things out, but he did.

I do know, because I now know him so well, what drove him to grow it once he started. If you could drive down costs and build a big enough position, you could make the play less like an oil and gas project and more like a manufacturing project. Performance up, costs down. It's an incredibly simple concept and Bill was one of the first--if not *the* first--in the industry to think it and then to do it.

By the 1990s, he had built his company into a half-billion dollar company with his name on the door, employed hundreds of people, took the company public, and ended up selling it, which eventually sold to a large independent and the asset he put together became one of their most important assets. Everyone thought he was crazy, but he was right.

When you do that, you don't need a resume and you get to bring your wife to dinner if that's what you want to do.

So, after fifteen years away from the business, he had decided to do it again. Different play this time, but the same concept. People didn't see what he saw. They didn't see the potential and what's more amazing (to me in particular), was that he was so confident that he was doing it with his own money. All of it. It didn't even cross his mind that he shouldn't. "Risk? Are you kidding? Investing in everybody else is a risk. I'm investing in myself." I must admit, I cannot argue with that logic. He was looking to take his plan bigger. StartUpCo could have been the platform, and that explains why he was at the dinner.

So why was Sandra there? Bill's wife is his partner. True in every sense of the word. They compare notes on business ideas and on life. They support each other. They make decisions together. And they didn't care what the world thought; she was at the dinner to evaluate me and be part of Bill's decision to join StartUpCo. I now get it and I now know why. Teammates are great, and sometimes, they are your spouse.

I credit them with showing me to be less afraid to be myself and to hell with what others want me to be. Trust your path and ignore what people think about you. Do what you think is right and if you turn people off, awesome. No energy required to be anything you aren't. Those that like you may love you, and those that love you will do anything for you. Deal with it.

So, dinner ends and two very different discussions happened. Bill and Sandra decided this was the role for them. The business plan was weak, but it could be changed. I .... Strike that.... We.... have to work with David!

At the same time as they were having that conversation, I called Michael to give him an update. Day three of my employment (that makes me laugh as I write this). The conversation went something like this.

Michael: How'd it go?

Me: Great. I love him. I would love to work with him. He's the man.

Michael: Awesome, I'll tell him tomorrow.

Me: Oh, sorry, wait. I don't mean hire him. You can't hire him. You two won't get along at all.

Michael: Excuse me, what? You said you love him. I think he's great too.

Me: Yes, I do. But you two can't work together. I'm young and I don't want to run this company right now. This is your deal, so unless you want him to run it, which includes him being your boss, he's not going to be happy. He understands YOUR business plan perfectly, he just thinks it's not going to work. You two will fight for power. He will quit because you are the founder and I will leave with him. So, unless you want to be CFO, not CEO, don't hire him.

The next day Michael and Bill and Sandra met. Bill and Sandra were ready to move to Denver, but Michael tells him "We aren't going to move forward." Bill is perplexed. "We had an awesome dinner. We believed the same things. And now we aren't going to do this together?" What kind of a sociopath must David be? What the F@&K is wrong with him?!?

Bill called me to ask, which I respect and admire so much, and had he not done that, I'm not sure we ever would have seen each other again. But he did. And we have.

Bill: Why did you tell Michael not to hire me?

I told him exactly what I told Michael….

David: I think you are awesome. I would love to work with you. But you can't work for Michael. It's not right. It won't work. It will kill you. You know what you want. You want to raise money and rebuild your company. Do that. Not here. It will work out.

Bill, Sandra, and I still talk about that dinner and talk about the juxtaposition of my knowing it wouldn't work with Bill and Michael but somehow believing I could make it work for me. Something about red flags being red flags, even if you were just fired rings a bell. I wonder who said that?

Flash forward ten months after that dinner and StartUpCo was in chaos and bleeding money. The business plan had totally failed. Lurching and laying-off the few people we had, leaving just me and Michael, waiting to run out of money. During that time, Bill put his money to work. He turned a $2 million into $10 million mark to market (as you should have learned by now, in oil and gas the best way to make money is to buy a dollar for 20 cents and the rest takes care of itself). Bill did find a partner, but they broke, split the company in two and at the time he needed someone to help him rebuild his model to figure out what he was going to do for cash. That was when he called me.

I took the gig for an hourly rate on the side. I had the time, I had the passion, I had the skill, and so I founded Prevail Energy, my consulting business. We started working together. I started co-investing in his deals. And the river started to pull me in a different direction than I expected it would.

Back to sitting on the plane in this cramped middle seat, typing like a madman and scaring the people beside me (perhaps they think THEY will be a chapter in the book. Nah, just a sentence). We are flying to New York to get a check for $30 million from a diversified institution. They want to give him more, but he thinks the strategy is best done small. He's brought his old CFO and the three of us are going to try to scale this business.

I reflect on the disaster that was StartUpCo- the planning, the process, the thinking- I find it ironic that we are doing the exact opposite. Three guys that don't yet officially work together, flying to New York to get a check to start a business. What's that saying: "If you have to pick up the phone more than once to raise money, you shouldn't be raising money?" Who said that? Must be a smart guy.

On the subject of Bill, collectively we both love golf and perhaps through the sport I can share the essence of a good coach or mentor.

There are times in your life when you lose sight of the forest for the trees and having someone that you trust to give you a nudge is a huge advantage. I've been so fortunate to have had several of them over the course of my life and career, and each has helped move me down the river and past an obstacle.

I'm a good golfer— a 0 handicap—which makes me a pretty good amateur player, yet eons away from being a pro. Bill's a 2 handicap. He took up golf later in life--after he sold his company--so he has always ruminated deeply about it, which is a much different approach than a young person learning the game. Young people "just do", older people think about "the why."

When we golf together, he watches me. I can hit shots that he can't hit. I can work the ball from left to right or from right to left. I can hit it high. I can hit it low. I can execute and I have the tools.

So, when I hit a shot with a skill that Bill doesn't have, he doesn't ask me about the skill. He questions me about why I am hitting that particular shot.

"You saw a draw to that pin?"

"Yeah, over the bunker, trouble left, wanted to leave it left of the pin worst and on the pin best."

"Hmm. Okay, interesting, I hadn't seen that shot."

The next time I have a similar shot, I line up for a fade. I hit the shot; I end up in trouble.

"Why did you hit the fade? You hit the draw earlier and it worked out great."

"I just wanted to hit it differently."

"You should have hit the draw."

That's good coaching. Observe, take note. Observe, correct.

On the last round we were playing, I was within inches of two hole-in-ones in the same round. I've never had a single hole-in-one, much less two. Actually, that's not totally true. In my mind, I did have a "hole-in-one" when I was sixteen…I hit a shot, airmailed the green, and lost the ball. I yelled to my dad, with whom I was playing at the time, "Throw me another ball." He did. The second ball went into the hole. My dad, always the comedian, replied "Nice 3."

Back to the round with Bill and I were playing. I was -1 through nine holes. Playing great, making putts, and hitting the ball exactly where I want. Almost had two hole-in-ones, after all.

On the tenth hole, I hit my worst drive of the day. Out of bounds on the left. Took a 6. The next hole a made a par 3. On the twelfth hole, I had an even worse swing than on the tenth and hit it out of bounds on the right.

Bill looks at me and says, "Who was that guy?"

I look blankly at him. I was fuming. I can't believe I just did that. I was playing amazingly, thinking about turning pro. I might be in the final group at the Masters next year. Then, two horrible swings later and I'm an amateur again.

I sit in the cart sulking. Bill says, "Why did you line up in the middle of the tee box?"

"I don't know."

"Why don't you line up on the right side of the tee box? You like the draw. Your error is the draw. If you hit it right, you're out of bounds anyway. So, aim right, and make sure you hit that little fucking ball down the middle."

I finished out the round with two birdies and two almost birdies.

The lesson: Bill didn't try to hit the shots and he didn't want to know how to hit the shots. He knew that I knew how to hit the shots, and that I had the tools, but he knew something I didn't. That is mentorship and why it's good to have one at the right time.

Lesson Seventeen

What They Don't Teach You in Business School

My wife and I had a number of couples over for dinner last week, including a couple we have known for eight years. We worked together in Canada and I helped get him to Denver for work. We talked about the last year and a half pretty candidly and he sent me a text later that week that said:

"Hey man. Forgot to tell you it was good to catch up. We both thought you looked fit and happy."

This line actually does get a chapter, the last chapter even, because it brought purpose and closure for me in regard to what this book was about. I hope that you have gained some value from my experiences, and I truly hope that you never have to be fired to get set on a new course. But, for me, when I liken myself today to the person I was eighteen months ago, there is no comparison, and that is the most important lesson in this book.

Now, we both know that the books that win Pulitzer prizes don't start out with the author thinking "I'm going to write a book that wins the Pulitzer prize." We also know that THIS author was only thinking "What the F@&K am I writing a book?" and we both know this isn't winning a prize for anything. I just needed to write it.

In a similar context, it is unrealistic and unfair to yourself to expend emotional capital on the belief that you are going to have a career that looks like "X." The fact is that you don't know what it's going to look like and that's the best part of the adventure, or at least I have found it to be once I stopped trying to get where I thought I was supposed to be going. All we can do is point ourselves in a direction and start walking.

As you now know, I had no idea I would end up "here", having been fired, having a failed business plan, and now what looks like it will be a successful one with a partner, coach, and friend. Maybe the biggest lesson is that things have a way of working out, if given long enough.

I truly thought I was happy when my career was on fire, when I had 300 emails a day, when I was busy and important with work things, and when my Blackberry was used for actual work--not Fantasy Football and watching YouTube videos. I was stressed out, surrounded by politics, and working my ass off to change the company and, for that matter, the world. And I truly thought it was worth it.

But over the last eighteen months, I have been blessed with the opportunity to stand back from what I was doing and the things I had lost sight of. During this process, for the first time since I've met the friend that sent the text earlier in the chapter, I'm really happy. Moreover, I think I've learned something about the work world that I couldn't see when I was standing in the forest.

This is my takeaway. In the beginning, I was a high-flying future CEO that had the world by the tail and with an incredible resume of experience and a deep hunger to become that CEO. If you've ever seen a resume, you have basically seen it: It can be distilled down.

David Ramsden-Wood, (Degree), (Degree)

Senior Executive; noted traits: time management, communication, problem solving.

Really good at work.

***

Candidly, I admit that though there were more words and descriptions of "amazing" things I had done, that was basically it. Really good at work. What wasn't written: Really bad at everything else.

It was what defined me and to me, your reading it meant you knew everything you needed to know about me.

Now, eighteen months later, here's what my resume looks like.

DRW

Father. Drops my kids off and picks them up from school.

Coach. U8 hockey- two teams; head coach; six hours per week. Squash. U15 young man who wants to play on a collegiate team one day, maybe Princeton.

PTA. That stands for parent teacher association (I didn't know either). I'm in charge of fundraising for my kids' school and I've set the goal to try to raise $500,000 between now and when my youngest son leaves in five years. I think I may be the first person to have given a speech at Parents Night that included value proposition and linked the value appreciation (or depreciation) of their home to having a top school in the neighborhood.

Friend. I have them. And I like them. And I like when we hang out or watch football or chase after kids (ours usually) in the park.

Husband. I'm still married. Against all odds. We're going to France next year.

Business owner. I consult to a number of clients and with my partner, Bill, we started a company.

Author. I finished my book. It won't win a Pulitzer. It may not get published. But it's done and so I can go on calling myself an author.

It's been eighteen months since "the event" (I don't even capital it anymore). I've learned a lot and I feel blessed to be doing what I love and what I'm good at AND be more balanced in my approach to life. I have no idea if I'm going to be financially successful, but I do know that I'm the happiest I've been in a very long time, and let's be honest: that kind of success is really the only kind that matters.

Here are a few final thoughts:

Money is precious Raise it when you don't need it, don't use it if you can avoid it. Money is expensive and money is power. If you give money, you should get power in proportion to the money you put in.

Partner with people you like It takes too much time and energy to start a company and simultaneously figure your partners out. Too many important discussions are left unsaid in the early days, and those discussions always end up in hindsight to have been extremely important. Have your say and get to a resolution. Ask the question "Can I live with it?" If the answer is no, you should deal with it.

Do what you know When you do what you know, you know what you don't. When you know what you don't, you can figure out how to solve that issue. It's easier to raise money, it's easier to run the business, and it's easier to change the plan when something isn't working.

Do what you love I have lost a lot money from people who are very close to me. And I don't like it. But I can look them in the eyes (or at least I assume I will be able to when the time comes) and tell them that I did everything I could to make this successful. I stuck with it because I love to do what I do, and I will stick to it despite the failure because I love doing what I do. I don't believe that my chances of starting a business are better now with one failure under my belt, but I do believe that my chances are better with all the learnings under my belt.

Never, never, never give up Starting a business is hard. Working for people is hard. Life is hard. Just put your head down, trust yourself, do your best and keep slogging. You never know when your big break is going to come.

I used to think that success in your career was the only thing that mattered. Friends, family, and life could take a backseat. When things were bad, you had to grin and bear it, but you would survive, and be better for it.

I no longer believe that. Life is short and hard enough as it is. Happiness is something that is attainable, and I have come to believe that that's the only kind of success that really matters. Because when you are happy, you make the people around you happy. And when people are happy, they really don't care how F@&Ked up you are. And I am a deeply F@&Ked up person. But it's okay. So are you. ☺

I am more productive today than I was when I was consumed by work.

I am happier now than I was when I was consumed by work.

And though I promise I can (and do, when required) work more hours and spend more time thinking about work than the average bear, I do it in a healthy way; in a way that respects balance, need, and productivity. And quite frankly, I know enough to say "Are you kidding me? What the F@&K is wrong with you?"

Take a step back. Reflect on your life and make the decisions that make YOU happy. The only constant in the human experience is you. You are who you wake up with, go to sleep with, and hang out all day every day with. Sure, you meet some nice people along the way. Some relationships last, some don't. But there you still are. You can lie to yourself, be angry with yourself, love, hate, admire or be disappointed in yourself and the next day, you wake up. Still you. Still there. It isn't like that with anybody else.

We have developed coping mechanisms that allow us to externalize and see things in others that protect us from them that we simply don't see in ourselves. How many times have friends or family members told you about their jobs or their relationships and you instantly knew the answer? You need to change jobs. Go on a trip with your partner. Buy a house in the mountains and live happily ever after. Ta Da! Fixed.

But when it comes to ourselves, we don't have that kind of clarity. We want to look outside ourselves to all the things everyone else has done with us or to us and make things better. The reality is that you are in charge of your life. It's time to take charge.

Whether it was through the process of writing this "memoir", because I grew as a person, because I found my life path, or because I am finished the book, I am happy. Really happy. And it's nice to be back.

So, the book that started out as a title and a chapter, then morphed through an angry and confused diatribe, has become something that was very useful for me and I hope it is for you, too.

So, what the F@&K <u>is</u> wrong with everybody else?

The answer I have come to discover is nothing. Absolutely nothing. And the sooner we get our head around that fact, the better we become. I wish you the best of luck in your own journey. And more than that, I wish you happiness. It's worth it.

Really Good Lines

Hope is not a plan.

A city isn't great, unless it's great for everyone (thanks mom)

When you are in the details all the time, you don't notice your ass is exposed by politics (thanks George)

It takes a woman nine months to make a baby. Nine women can't make a baby in a month.

Every deal worth doing dies twice.

If you need to pick up the phone more than once to raise money, you probably shouldn't be raising money.

Never ever ever give up.

Epilogue: Losing Weight, Revisited

Karma. It is fitting that we end the book where we started: Losing weight. Work had consumed my love of exercise. And without exercise, the body begins to change. Slowly. Daily. Almost unnoticeably. But change it does.

It starts small, of course. Your favorite t-shirt starts to accentuate different parts of your body. You slough it off. "Water retention," you explain, "I had a really salty meal yesterday and flew last week. No big deal."

The pockets on your dress pants start to flare. The button above the zipper is starting to pull at your waist, and usually hand-in-hand, you are afraid to bend over to pick something up. You sort of kick it along with your foot and maneuver as though you are examining a relic of history.

Finally, there is the defining moment--at least if you are a guy--when one of your closest friends says, "Hey David, want me to buy you some sweatpants?"

That's when you have the first, good, long, naked look at yourself in the mirror and you say "What the F@&K!" For me that happened December 20th.

While I would like to state that my size gain was related to something to do with a demonstration, I cannot. I got lazy; I drank too much; I ate whatever I wanted; I always had dessert. I actually knew from experience that a peanut butter bagel for a post dinner snack didn't go well with wine unless you cleansed the palate with a Reese's Peanut Butter cup in between! Irony is rich, and so it was that I would have to prove myself right or eat my words. Fortunately, I was the size that if need be, I could.

I needed to lose weight. Ugh, that sounds truly awful. You can choose to ignore what has been creeping up on you for months or you can begin to plan the next few months of absence, longing, fatigue and a state I like to refer to as perma-hunger. In this state, everything, including brussel sprouts, begins to look very appealing.

So, on December 20th, I devised a four-step plan to do just that.

Step 1 Eat less.

Step 2 Exercise more.

Step 3 Make an extremely public bet with a very competitive friend and, the key

Step 4 Eat like a motherF@&Ker between December 20th and the weigh in date of January 1st.

Let's start with step 3. The bet.

The public commitment is a powerful, yet seldom used, tool to help bolster your cause. From the first time I saw the Seinfeld "*Master of your Domain*" episode, I realized the brilliance of a public and shameful bet. Such a bet requires two things: A great subject – in this case losing X% of body weight between two dates and, secondly, a great person with whom to bet.

Enter Ken. Mister Sweatpants himself.

"Okay, smartass. You and me. January 1st to March 15th. Total percentage of body weight loss."

"You're on."

Now, for true success, the prize must be worth fighting for. Monetary rewards are fine, but I liked the gift certificate better at work, so it needed to be an "experience" bet. It needed to be a bet that would captivate those that knew of the bet, and encourage them to ask all the time "Who's winning?" It needed to be special.

The Bet: The loser hands their credit card over to the winner. The winner then uses said credit card to take out both the winner's and loser's spouses and the losing partners' best friend for a night of fine dining, theatre, dancing. No holds barred. No limits.

Oh yeah, and the loser says home and babysits the kids.

The other key on the bet was duration. This was no one month of abstinence from good food and fasting. It was a 75-day lifestyle changing bet. To win, you had to stay committed, and in that time, both participants--regardless of who wins--will have established and ingrained habits that will keep the health up and the weight down.

Step 4, an equally important part of this bet. Eat like it's your last ten days on Earth. Which is exactly what I did between December 20th and January 1st, the day of the weigh-in. I literally ate every bad thing that I had in the house--trail mix, booze, cookies, chocolate…you name it.

While this might seem like an odd step, it has a number of benefits:

1) You don't feel guilty about throwing food away, especially Oreo cookies. I love those things.
2) It's Christmas… are you kidding?! Are you really going to start a diet over Christmas when there is more food available than at any time of the year? Exactly.
3) Everyone "resolves" to do something January 1st. You can guarantee that for at least four days in January, none of your friends will be drinking or having parties, so you won't be faced with the dilemma that faces all dieters: How can I not eat that when it looks so good!?
4) It gives you adequate time to mentally prepare for perma-hunger and make some truly obnoxious comments to your fellow bettor or bettors to ensure your own compliance.

On January 1st, I weighed in at 224 lbs, my all-time high. This is what I did to win the bet by 1% and lose thirty pounds in 75 days and keep it off for the last four months (Yes, there is a maintenance bet until September 1st):

I downloaded an App for my iPhone that counted calories. I entered my current weight, activity level, height, and goal weight and it did the rest. The beautiful thing about this App is that it actually shows you the eight major "sources" of good (or bad.) Protein, Carbs, Sugar, Fat, Saturated fat, sodium, cholesterol and total calories. It's not only educational, it allows you to make better choices by knowing what you are eating.

As an aside, the App suggested for a man of 6'3, I should weigh between 172 and 192 lbs. I was 192 lbs when I was a professional athlete and twenty-two, so I'm going to call bullshit. But that's another chapter and not for this book.

For a man of my size and body weight, I burn somewhere between 2,200 and 2,800 calories a day just being alive. There are 3,500 calories in a pound. By knowing this and making good choices, it is pretty easy to keep your intake to below 2,000 calories per day which means that you will lose between 1,400 and 5,600 calories (about half a pound to a pound and a half) a week.

There are lots of ways to maximize your caloric burn rate which will increase your rate of weight loss. Pick the Starbucks that's a few blocks from your office or house and walk. Coffee has effectively no calories if you drink it black. Moreover, caffeine is a stimulant which increases your metabolic rate. Take the stairs instead of the elevator; get up from your desk and walk around the office. And my number one recommendation: Do twenty push-ups every morning the second you get out of bed. You do it every day. No matter how you are feeling. It lets you know how you are doing by comparison to every other day. Are you feeling tired? Sore? Do you need more sleep? More food? A day of rest? You get your heart rate up and remind yourself that you are working towards a goal.

The most important part, however, is that you enter the food into your App <u>before</u> you eat it. I don't know if this is a common thing, but I will tell you, when you are counting calories and you find out that one chocolate chip cookie is 150 calories and a Coors light is 90 calories, knowledge is power. I realized I can drink a beer over fifteen minutes (six calories a minute) and keep the beer ice cold and be 60 calories ahead of the cookie that I ate at 150 calories in one minute and subsequently crave a glass of milk to go with it for 110 calories more.

It is also amazing the things you learn about the foods you eat. For instance, milk has a lot of protein and sugar. Sugar is a carbohydrate and is burned by the body readily and quickly. Protein is the building block of muscle and takes longer to break down. So while milk is great for kids and a great source of protein, there are better alternatives like fat-free Greek yogurt. It has the same protein benefit and you can use it to replace the milk you would have with cereal. If you want a little more flavor, add some sugar-free vanilla flavor.

Eggs are a great source of protein and super easy to make, but they have a ton of cholesterol. With a recommended daily limit of 300 mg of per day, two scrambled whole eggs put you over that limit before 8 a.m. Some people suggest that you just have egg whites, but I think throwing away perfectly good and healthy food seems crazy. Be mindful. Be moderate.

For me, breakfast was a single scrambled egg, Greek yogurt mixed with Fiber 1 cereal, and fifteen frozen blueberries to add a bit of flavor and healthy carbohydrates. That's about 230 calories.

For the first month, I avoided eating bread to the degree possible so that I would be relatively lower in carbs and higher in protein. I ignored fat content entirely. When you eat healthy and are watching calories, I am not aware of any foods that fall in that category that are unduly high in fats.

Other food learnings before we get to exercise:

Juice has a ton of sugar. I couldn't figure out why this was the case until a nutritionist made me visualize how many individual fruits it takes to make a container… good point. I do have Pomegranate or other "Super Juices" at home, but I only drink a single four-ounce glass at a time, and usually as a snack or sometimes in the morning. There is just too much sugar, and if I'm going to have that much fruit, I'd prefer fermented grape juice, the red variety.

Cottage Cheese is the best food for protein and easily accessible for snacks. Low in fat. Low in carbohydrates.

Meal replacement drinks. Okay, I'm sure there are a lot of eye rolls for all the bad in them. Too much unnatural stuff. Maybe. But McDonald's has a lot of unnatural stuff too and between the two, I'll take a 200-calorie high protein low sugar drink over a 500 calorie burger. Don't get me wrong, I love burgers, but I honestly believe the key is to go balls to the wall for the first thirty days, then ease off a bit. The reason behind this is that you are the most motivated at the beginning AND you absolutely need to see results to get positive reinforcement.

Whey protein supplements can be used for snacks when you are at home. They are very low in sugar and fat, and the protein gives you energy. I find that I don't get nearly as stiff anymore after working out if I consume these. They recommend drinking thirty minutes before a workout and thirty minutes after, which I think mainly is to increase your consumption. I only do the after. Less overall calories and I want the protein to rebuild the muscle. I like to work out on an empty stomach so that my body goes straight to the fat stores.

Weigh yourself every day. I have kept a journal of my weight virtually every day. I know that the body changes weight 3-7 pounds a day based on meals, water retention, and sodium intake. But I also know that you can't manage what you don't measure. If you get on the scale every day and you drop weight, you feel rewarded. When you gain weight, and you know your calories in the material balance should not make that possible, you can reflect on what you ate or did to make your body respond that way.

Some might only want to see progress every week to get the average, but I believe if you have an up day in week three after a down day in week two and your weight loss was less than you expected, you can have a huge set back.

Cut your booze. My favorite question at the doctor, is "How many alcoholic beverages do you have a week?" I know very few who actually answer that question honestly. My friend did.

"How many drinks do you have a week?"

"Forty-two."

"I said a week."

"I heard you."

Don't get me wrong, I love to drink. But drinking contains a lot of calories. Most importantly, if you drink at lunch, you probably won't work out after that. You also are more likely to say "Well, today is written off. Oh well...." and eat worse than you otherwise would. Also, if you over-imbibe, you won't want to do push-ups the next morning and the train risks derailing. So, I reiterate--enter the drinks BEFORE you have them and have an intellectual debate as to whether you really want to have that drink.

I did cut out drinking entirely for the first five days (resolution time). That convinced me that I wasn't an alcoholic--a fun email to send my mom who spent the Christmas holidays telling me not to open more wine.

After that, I chose wine over beer, drank only with or after dinner, and alternated with water and tea. Tea has many of the same characteristics I'm fond of with the habit of drinking wine-sipping, sitting in a comfortable chair, wondering if you should make/have some more. Chopping up green onions with ginger and boiling it with water is a tasty, spicy mix that is actually good for you.

Exercise. I heard someone give advice that I thought was pretty good: "Go to the gym every day. Even if you don't work out. You will get in the habit of going and eventually you will think it's a waste of time just to go and not do anything and eventually, you will work out." Hey, if it works....

If you have gained weight to the point where you actively want to lose it, I'm going to go out on a limb that you probably weren't working out that much. I know that I wasn't. If you've always "had a weight problem," I'm going to go out on a limb and say you probably didn't learn "how to train."

I was fortunate as a kid in that my parents kept me out of parties, drugs, and alcohol with sports. It was always there. I was involved with many sports until I was fourteen and then I chose one upon which to focus. I trained for two to three hours a day and basically lived at the club where I trained. I learned "how to train" by training with other people who already knew "how to train." So, if you don't know "how to train", I'm going to explain it.

Training is awful. You learn where the limits of your body are. You should throw up after training at least once. That's as hard as you can work… Though I would recommend getting a base layer of fitness before trying it. The only reason in sports to train is so that when you compete, you don't have to work nearly as hard to win. That's it. If you are losing, you train harder, so you don't lose, and eventually, you won't have to work that hard to win. So, you should not be happy when you are training. You should be pushing yourself. Hard. And the harder you push, the faster you get fitter, the more you lose weight, the fitter you get, the better you feel. You win.

Pushing yourself is hard for some people. Even for me. And you convince yourself that you are pushing yourself, but you probably find a gear that looks hard, but you know isn't. For this, I highly recommend classes. When I was competing, I didn't need the extra motivation because once every couple weekend, I was in a tournament. That pushed me. I hate losing. But when you are losing weight, regardless of the bet, there isn't really a "tournament." You can slack some days, and no one will notice. You will still lose weight, but again, I say, people want results. They want to see results. Feel the results. Soon. The harder you work while you are motivated, the faster you lose weight and the better able you will find continuing to motivate yourself.

So, back to classes. I went to the first spin class I have ever been to yesterday. That was crazy. I'm happy to hop on a stationary bike and work hard for twenty minutes. Maybe thirty. But an hour?!? No way would I do that by myself. With fifteen other people, however, I make it a goal to work harder and stay longer than them. My first spin class, I burned 1,050 calories according to the bike computer during that hour. The instructor did 850 calories. I know that in our next class he will want to beat me. I will make sure to tell him I don't intend to lose. When you say things like that, it makes it harder to slack off.

I also started doing yoga. I think flexibility is the worst thing to work on but the easiest thing to improve and it has the most impact in regard to the way you feel. Knee pain, back pain, shoulder tightness. We all have it… spending an hour just stretching makes me feel like I am delaying aging. I'm not a yoga guy. In fact, I don't tell anyone I do it. I just do it and I feel better. My back hurts less, my knees feel great, and I have more bounce in my step.

There is no magic formula. I hope I have given you some thoughts and that some of the thoughts will work for you. I can tell you though that there is no reason you can't lose weight. Make a bet. Be very public about it. Eat less. Exercise more.

Sadly, it is that ~~easy~~ hard.

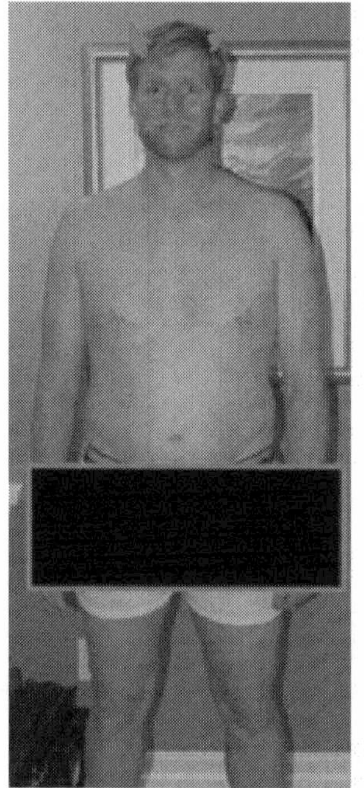

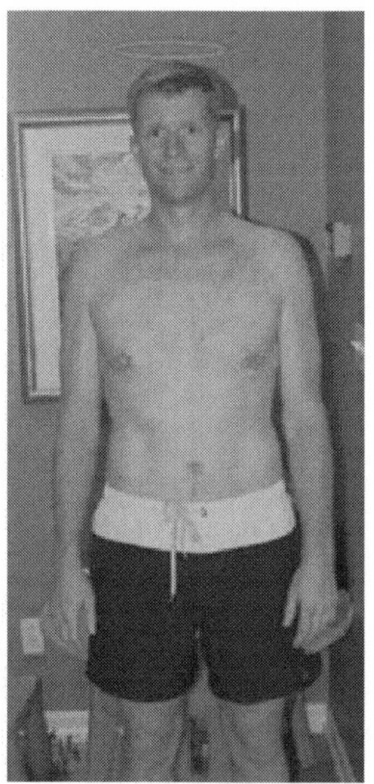

The Change from January 1 to March 15. Thirty pounds.

Acknowledgements

First and foremost, my family. All of them. For living all the stories that I write about; for sticking with me in the darkest days, and for everything they have done to make me, me. Mom, Dad, Ashley, Tara, Benjamin, and Andrew. I love you guys.

To my in-laws. Yes, you can claim me in your "firing ledger."

To my editors. Thank you for trudging. It's true, I don't know where apostrophes go.

To my most loyal boosters. Our company will be incredible, and I'm sorry I let you down. I promise, I'm a lot better for it.

To my friends. You know who you are. Thank you for your wisdom and patience and laughter.

To Tara. You saved my life. More than once. Thank you.

Manufactured by Amazon.ca
Bolton, ON